D0996785

THE CORPORATE BRAND

Withdrawn from
Queen Margaret University Library

QUEEN MARGARET UNIVERSITY
COLLEGE LIBRARY

The Corporate Brand

Nicholas Ind

© Nicholas Ind 1997

All rights reserved. No reproduction, copy or transmission of this publication may be made without written permission.

No paragraph of this publication may be reproduced, copied or transmitted save with written permission or in accordance with the provisions of the Copyright, Designs and Patents Act 1988, or under the terms of any licence permitting limited copying issued by the Copyright Licensing Agency, 90 Tottenham Court Road, London W1P 9HE.

Any person who does any unauthorised act in relation to this publication may be liable to criminal prosecution and civil claims for damages.

The author has asserted his right to be identified as the author of this work in accordance with the Copyright, Designs and Patents Act 1988.

First published 1997 by
MACMILLAN PRESS LTD
Houndmills, Basingstoke, Hampshire RG21 6XS
and London
Companies and representatives
throughout the world

ISBN 0–333–67472–3

A catalogue record for this book is available
from the British Library.

This book is printed on paper suitable for recycling and made from fully managed and sustained forest sources.

10 9 8 7 6 5 4
06 05 04 03 02 01 00

Copy-edited and typeset by Povey–Edmondson
Tavistock and Rochdale, England

Printed in Great Britain by
Creative Print & Design (Wales)
Ebbw Vale, Gwent

Contents

List of Figures, Tables and Boxes

Figures

Tables

Boxes

Preface

The idea for this book came from the observation that companies all too frequently segment the way they communicate. This tends to lead to fragmentation and confusion. Yet consumer and other audiences seem to prefer organisations that present themselves clearly and consistently. From primary and secondary research, as well as the experience of conducting consultancy projects, I came to the conclusion that addressing this problem requires recognition of the issue and also a corporate value system that supports action. The former is easy to achieve, the latter far harder. Companies can be consistent communicators through their advertising or direct marketing, but achieving continuity with the ideas and actions of individuals and the delivery of products and services needs widely understood and endorsed values. The is the heart of the idea of *The Corporate Brand.*

This book covers the environmental factors that are making corporate branding more important: more confident consumers who want to know more about the company behind a product or service, the rapid diffusion of technology that encourages product similarity, the globalisation of markets that has created a worldwide consumer base and the interest of a diverse number of interest groups and audiences in the activities of organisations. However, the work is more than just a commentary, it goes on to discuss the relationship of corporate branding to strategy and the means of analysing the corporate brand. Various audiences – employees, shareholders, the media and local communities – and their relationship to the corporate brand are observed and assessed. Finally the book goes on to look at the ways in which companies can manage the corporate brand most effectively.

The book concludes with the message that companies need to be good listeners if they are to balance and meet the needs of their various stakeholders.

To illuminate the arguments in the text I have introduced a wide-ranging number of examples. I hope this will help to bring the issues to life and to provide real-life examples as to how some of the ideas in the book can be – and are – put into practice.

NICHOLAS IND

Acknowledgements

The author and publishers acknowledge with thanks permission to reproduce the following copyright material: MORI, for Figures 1.1 and 2.1 and Table 4.1; Free Press, for Figure 3.1, from M. Porter, *Competitive Advantage: Creating and Sustaining Superior Performance* (1985); Landor Associates/Burton Marsteller, for Figure 4.3; Conference Board and Braxton Associates, for Figures 8.1 and 8.2; Jack Wood for Figure 9.1. Every effort has been made to contact all the copyright-holders, but if any have been inadvertently omitted, the publishers will be pleased to make the necessary arrangement at the earliest opportunity.

Abbreviations

ADR	American Depository Receipt
CAD	computer aided design
CAM	computer aided manufacture
CBI	Confederation of British Industry
CCI	Corporate Community Involvement
CEO	chief executive officer
CI	corporate identity
CRO	chief reputation officer
DTP	desk top publishing
EC	European Community
ERM	exchange rate mechanism
fmcg	fast moving consumer goods
GATT	General Agreement on Tariffs and Trade
IT	information technology
MIT	Massachusetts Institute of Technology
OECD	Organisation for Economic Cooperation and Development
ORC	Opinion Research Corporation
RSA	Royal Society of Arts
TI	Tube Investments

1 The Corporate Brand

Why are there so many television programmes, books, newspapers and magazines devoted to business? Partly it is because as consumers, employees, managers and shareholders, companies define, enrich and nurture (and occasionally damage) our lives. Business may not offer us the depth of experience of religion or family, but its influence is all-pervasive. Partly it is because business is a spectacle; it has drama and excitement and adventure. It's like the characters from the *Commedia dell'Arte* 'who display in their costumes and attitudes, the future contents of their parts'.[1] The actors do not just interact with each other, they get the audience on their side, or against them, by their willingness to fight fairly, by their integrity as individuals and by their gestures. We can 'read' the character of an actor, such as the Harlequin, from his actions and his looks. Similarly we 'read' a company by its outward signs, such as its advertising, its brochures and its reported performance. What interests us as an audience is the unfolding of the action; the posturing; the personifications of good and evil. It's IBM versus Apple, Boeing versus Airbus, British Airways versus Virgin, Coca-Cola versus Pepsi. Depending on our experience and image of the adversaries, and indeed our own sense of self, we identify with one or the other. For example, when Apple ran its 1984 campaign which presented IBM as Big Brother and Apple as the iconoclasts out to empower computer users, it was clear, at least to some, that IBM was the personification of evil. However, 'good' doesn't always triumph. IBM came to dominate the personal computer market and Microsoft the software market. Similarly British Airways is the big bruiser who wants to be liked, while Virgin is the underdog – the people's champion. Of course these judgements are simplistic and may not be based on reality. But this is also exactly the way that consumers and other audiences categorise organisations. There is a game you can play in research groups, when you ask the participants to associate organisations with animals or cars or people. The participants have no problems at all – even on very limited knowledge of making linkages; they read the signs, just as a theatre audience does. Companies that get categorised as rats or snakes tend not to have positive images.

So what can business learn from the *Commedia dell'Arte*? First, images determine people's attitudes and behaviour; a positive image can help create support for a company and its products. Second, that image is a mixture of appearance and action – the one needs to endorse the other. Third, to succeed one needs to be a good communicator. Last, it's not the transient ebbs and flows of the action that matter – it's having the skill and the resources to triumph in the end. It is the combination of performance and image that defines the successful corporate brand.

Definitions

Corporate branding is one of those things that everyone believes is important, yet there is very little consensus as to what it means. Words such as 'values', 'identity', 'image' and 'communication' swirl around. It is undoubtedly related to all these things. Some writers, such as John Balmer equate it with corporate identity: 'the strategic importance of corporate brand management (or what is more appropriately called strategic corporate identity management) would appear to be irrefutable.'[2] However the danger with linking corporate branding to the idea of corporate identity, even when it is prefixed by 'strategic' is that most audiences begin to think design and see logos. Therefore a distinct and clear definition of the corporate brand is required. Both the words 'corporate' and 'brand' carry certain connotations. 'Corporate' implies organisations – both profit and non-profit making – in their totality. It encompasses everything from the small family-run firm to the largest multinational. What defines it as corporate is its cohesion: the idea of people coming together and working towards a common goal. Thus, a corporate body has strategic decision making potential. In this definition, branch offices and divisions of a larger body are not corporate, unless they are responsible for determining strategy or have goals that are distinctively different from the parent company. However things – least of all definitions – are rarely this concise, and there are factors that serve to diffuse the meaning of 'corporate'. First, in many organisations, the common goal is not clearly defined and as a result sub-groups can develop their own, often contradictory, directions. In this context, trying to define what a particular corporation stands for can be very difficult. Second, organisations are not static objects, rooted in time and space. They evolve in response to the environment and as a consequence of the decisions they take. What may be our idea of an organisation at one point may prove to be erroneous later. Last, it is important to remember that no matter how the organisation defines itself and its decision making, there is still the potential for consumers and other stakeholders to see it differently. It is possible for the corporate definition of self and how it is perceived to be out of kilter, either because of deliberate policy or mismanagement. Although these caveats temper the definition of 'corporate', they do not undermine it. Rather it suggests that we need to understand an organisation and its structure in depth, before making judgements about it.Traditionally a 'brand' is a descriptor applied to the sort of fast-moving consumer goods one buys from a supermarket. It is distinct from the simple idea of a product in that there is a suggestion in the notion of a brand of values that go beyond mere functional performance. As Stephen King says, in the preface to his book *Developing New Brands*, 'a product is something that is made, in a factory; a brand is something that is bought, by a customer.[3] A product can be copied by a competitor; a brand is unique.'

It is the joining together of these two words – corporate and brand – that suggests a new way of looking at organisations. There is still the temptation to think of the visual presentation and the immediate reaction is to see company names and logos. These are the most overt signs of an organisation and this indicates why the management of a company's visual identity is so important. Nonetheless we should not mistake the sign for the substance. For example, Apple Computers is more than its name and its Garden of Eden apple. It is a company with a history, a set of values, a reputation and a strategy for the future, managed and worked for by people. In Stephen King's terminology, the Apple is something that is 'bought' by a wide variety of audiences: everyone from shareholders to employees to consumers.

Historically the marketing of brands has dominated marketing literature and thinking. This has been because most academic marketing courses have been focused on brands, as have the texts to support them. Consequently, all too often the enterprise behind the brand has been in the shadows. Now there are good reasons why the enterprise should be in the sun. However, before we blindly accept the pre-eminence of corporate marketing, we need to understand what it is and to recognise there are subtle differences between it and brand marketing. There are three core attributes that define the corporate brand as a distinct area:

- intangibility
- complexity
- responsibility.

Intangibility

The writer Iris Murdoch notes:

> We see parts of things, we intuit whole things. We seem to know a great deal on the basis of very little . . . We fear plurality, diffusion, senseless accident, chaos, we want to transform what we cannot dominate or understand into something reassuring and familiar.[4]

When we buy a consumer brand, such as a shampoo, we can touch, feel and smell it. We may not know or understand its chemical make-up, but we can describe its attributes with a fair degree of certainty. Although a brand will have some intangible elements a company is far more remote. Unless we work for a company, we rarely know much about its history, strategy, values and culture. We glean information from its communications, its people and its products and we make judgements. We decide that Shell is a good company and BP is not, or vice versa. Similarly our ideas change. When Shell is funding the revitalisation of our inland waterways it's a good company, but when it is planning to sink the Brent Spar oil platform out at sea, it's a bad company. Both judgements are simplistic. Shell like all companies makes good and bad decisions, but because we lack an intimate understanding of the company, our attitudes alter depending on the information we have available. (Shell's reputation declined noticeably following Brent Spar. The researcher, MORI, asked people if the company took its social responsibilities seriously. The measure which had been consistent for a number of years fell by nearly 10 percentage points as a direct result of its confrontation with Greenpeace.) In market research into companies, consumer assumptions and beliefs rarely withstand scrutiny. If a respondent claims a certain image for a company, the basis of the view is often shallow and deeply influenced by media coverage. Nonetheless, in spite of this superficiality, people can be deeply motivated by corporate actions – certainly the boycotting of Shell and attacks on petrol stations over Brent Spar was vociferous. It is, as Murdoch suggests, our need to transform plurality into order and familiarity that encourages us to construct the information we receive whatever its validity into something we can understand in our own terms. This echoes Sartre's view that we feel alien in a world without meaning, so therefore we have to create meaning ourselves. We select what is relevant to our lives and interpret it from our own perspective. Our views are determined by our culture, society, upbringing and plain self-interest. When the former Governor of Hong Kong, Chris Patten, was a

Conservative MP and member of the Cabinet, he was against the idea of providing citizenship rights to 3 million Hong Kong Chinese. After resigning his parliamentary seat and becoming Governor, his allegiances switched and he announced himself in favour of granting citizenry. A duplicitous or a genuine turnaround? Being generous, one might judge that the same problem viewed from several thousand miles apart looks rather different.

There is, then, an important difference between the reality of an organisation and its image. We see and hear a company's messages and experience its products or people and out of this miasma we construct an image that may, or may not, bear a close relationship to what the organisation actually is. Image then is a personal experience, but it is also collective. Although our deeper views about a specific organisation may vary, what can be observed from quantitative research is the collective view. When an organisation says it has an image as professional, innovative and dynamic, what it means is that a majority of external audiences subscribe to this view. It will still be possible to find people who believe exactly the opposite. There is a general truism that familiarity equates to favourability (Figure 1.1), but within that truism there are a great variety of viewpoints. There are then no absolutes, merely a collection of messages that form together in our minds to create an idea of an organisation and what it does.

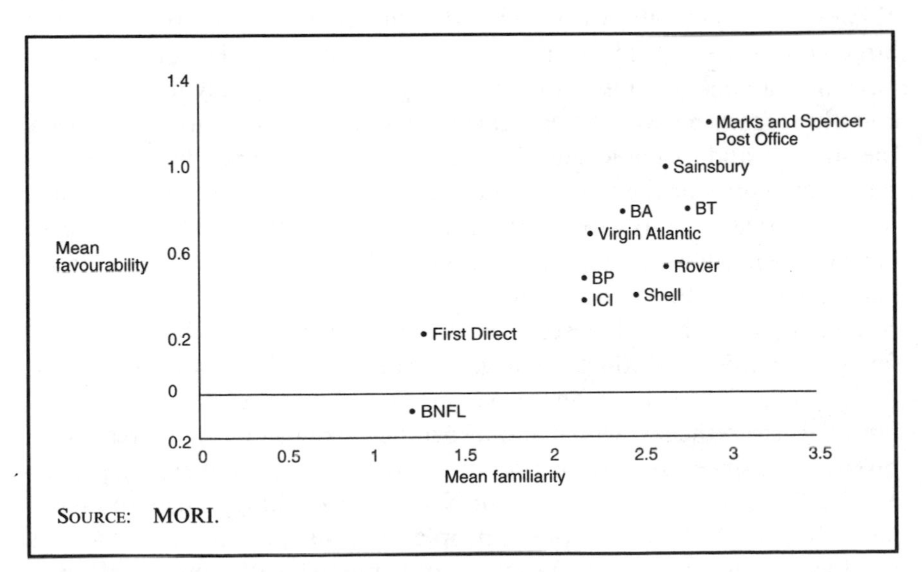

SOURCE: MORI.

Figure 1.1 Company familiarity and favourability, general public, November 1995

Getting to grips with a corporate brand is a difficult task and requires relevant communication. To create tangibility, communication should work at two levels. First, while accepting that each individual will have a unique idea of the organisation, there is still the need to try to build a consensual image that is both an accurate representation and also helps the fulfilment of corporate strategy. This requires consistency of communication to all stakeholders. Second, at the micro level, the organisation needs to build interactive relationships on a one-to-one basis with each individual stakeholder, whether they be customer, supplier or investor.

Building relationships

For a small business the idea of tangible relationships is axiomatic. A good high street butcher, for example, will know the names of his customers and their requirements. He will get special orders for them and tell them about special cuts of meat. He will know his suppliers and discuss his requirements with them. If hc is sensible he will know his bank manager, provide him with information on the business and seek advice when he needs to. He will probably know and talk to his main competitors and he may belong to a trade association. For the butcher, knowing his stakeholders and understanding their needs allows him to compete with the buying power of the large supermarket groups. However, there is no reason why the supermarket groups and other large companies should not pursue a similar strategy. Historically they have not done so because as with all large businesses they have become complex organisms with bureaucracies that have put up barriers between the strategy and its implementation. Unlike the high street butcher it has not been viable for the Chief Executive of a national supermarket chain to have a relationship with all the company's stakeholders. The process has been delegated and in its delegation diluted. Also the dictates of mass marketing and the concern with market share have dictated that companies have been focused on volume, based essentially on selling fairly standardised products to large numbers of undifferentiated people. In reality consumers have always wanted products tailored to their needs, but apart from the few who could afford bespoke products, the reality of production, since the introduction of the machine age and Henry Ford's Model T, has been standardisation. Now the technology exists to create individual products for individual people. It exists to tailor the process of production and it exists to monitor and interact with consumers. For example, in automotive engineering, developments in electronics means that a car can be tailored by the customer to determine such aspects as the ride height, steering, gear change points, brakes, aerodynamics and performance:

> What makes a Chevrolet a Chevrolet will no longer be defined by a preconception of the engineers, but by an individual's expression of what it should be. This in turn means that auto makers will stop trying to outguess groups of consumers about what they really want the steering to feel like. Their goal instead will be to enlarge the range of choices from which customers can themselves select what they want.[5]

The ability of companies to tailor products has the potential to attract new customers but, more importantly, it has the power to retain and develop existing customers. In certain markets, where since the 1970s capacity has been outstripping demand (cars, steel, trucks, airlines, shipbuilding, textiles), the value of keeping the customers you already have is paramount. This has heralded a boom in loyalty cards, bonus schemes and direct marketing initiatives, aimed at what Don Peppers and Martha Rogers in their book *The One to One Future*[6] call 'share of customer'. They and others argue that it is the potential long-term value of a customer that is important, not a one-off purchase, which is often expensive to obtain. The value to Ford of a first-time Fiesta buyer is not the cost of the car, but the potential lifetime spend and the benefit of word of mouth endorsement if the product performs. The challenge for the company is to spot the best potential source of long-term customer relationships and, having acquired them, to nurture them. Inevitably there are costs and rewards involved in building a relationship and companies need to determine the value exchange:

> the relationship between the financial investment a company makes in particular customer relationships and the return that customers generate by the specific way in which they choose to respond to the company's offer.[7]

In most businesses, the long-established idea of the Pareto effect – that 20% of your customers provide 80% of your business – applies. The primary task for business should be to retain and develop that 20% through specific and relevant offers. The negative aspect of this concentration on core customers is that certain customers become effectively disenfranchised; they lose their ability to consume. This has already started to happen within the insurance industry, whereby insurers will not cover home contents in certain inner-city locations in the UK. Although this may make commercial sense, in other markets, such as retail and air travel, it has the potential to exclude the 20%ers of the future. Loyalty rewarders therefore need to think carefully about the attitudes and behaviour patterns they encourage.

The idea of making an organisation tangible through relationships – as with the high street butcher – can and should go beyond consumers. The Royal Society of Arts (RSA) (1995) research project into British Business, *Tomorrow's Company*, which involved face to face consultations with 8000 business leaders and opinion formers, stated as its overall vision that:

> The companies which will sustain competitive success in the future are those which focus less exclusively on shareholders and on financial measures of success – and instead include all their stakeholder relationships.

It goes on to recommend that 'tomorrow's company',

> Works actively to build reciprocal relationships with customers, suppliers and other key stakeholders through a partnership approach.

The reality is that the RSA report found that very few companies in Britain are truly world class (although most think they are), and that part of the reason for this is the failure to build relationships with all of a company's stakeholders. This is partly a British cultural legacy, but it is also due to the failure of businesses everywhere to integrate all their business relationships in a company-wide strategy based on a common vision. In other words although the technology may now exist to enable organisations to build relationships with all stakeholders, the enabling culture does not. Yet it is only through a relationship-based approach to all of a company's activities that an organisation can achieve meaning for the individual, can communicate in a way that is uniquely relevant to each person.

Complexity

The second key differential between brands and corporate brands is the issue of complexity. Companies can include several decision making bodies, numerous operating divisions, large numbers of products and thousands of people. This makes control very difficult. With a physical brand and to a lesser extent a service brand, continuity of experience is achievable. Within a corporate brand it is much harder to attain. A company can contain several different cultures. David Potter, Chairman of laptop computer manufacturer, Psion says:

> the people within Psion are quite a broad church . . . the psychology and culture of the software nerd is utterly different from corporate sales. I'm not even sure they speak the same language. The one is a vulcan, the other is an earthling. The classic sales person needs a BMW, needs the money to look elegant and his main weapon in his personal armoury is charm. This is total anathema to the software person: he is not driven by money, he is driven by self-esteem and peer group esteem and the excitement at being at the front of somcthing.[8]

The individual who buys a Psion product will probably not appreciate this diversity, but buyers and suppliers, depending on their point of contact with the organisation, will have different perceptions. In addition to the problems of cultural diversity, corporate brand complexity develops through the naming structures that companies use to either link business units or products together under one banner (Sony, Yamaha) or not, as in the case of Procter & Gamble, which sells a number of seemingly unrelated brands.The latter is fairly typical of fast-moving consumer goods companies that often want to put competing products on to the market without the consumer knowing they come from the same stable. However, in the face of competition from own-label, some manufacturers such as Unilever have started to defend their corner through the use of corporate naming on packs. This has two potential benefits. It achieves economies of communication, in that all of a company's products support each other through a common endorsement, in much the same way that the Sony brand name adds value to its full product range. Second, the use of corporate naming helps to communicate to professional audiences, such as investors, the strength of the company's brand portfolio. But, if nothing is done to establish the corporate brand behind the name – the sum of values that represents the organisation – the addition of the company name to a product in itself achieves very little. This is a much more complex area and involves communication to all of a company's audiences.

Just as corporate branding is more complex than traditional brand marketing, so is communications. The way an audience builds up an awareness of a company is multifaceted. It occurs through the overt means of communication, such as advertising, literature, press coverage and direct marketing as well as the actions and behaviour of individuals. If the company name is used on products, such as BMW or Apple, the direct experience – or at least sight – of the product will be a key factor in our attitude towards the organisation. In most contexts where we buy the product will impinge on our views of it. As will the after sales service and support. Finally, but probably most importantly, the leaders and employees who represent the company will colour our beliefs about it – and the latter will also be recipients of many of the above forms of communication. This suggests that if the picture we have of an organisation is to have clarity, all of these forms of communication need to work cohesively together. Recipients of communication, by and large, will not differentiate the source of information. They may admire the advertising in its own right, but generally the messages a company emits are combined in an unconscious way to form an image. This is as true for the consumer as for the institutional investor and for the journalist. Indeed although one tends to separate out all of the audiences of a company for analytical purposes there will be overlap – the journalist may also be a consumer, the employee an investor.

The problem for many organisations is that communications are compartmentalised: corporate affairs talks to financial audiences; marketing talks to consumers; and human relations talks to employees. Even within marketing in large organisations different people will commission direct marketing activity, public relations, design and advertising. Unless there is a powerful integrative force the possibilities for fragmentation are enormous. It needs glue to hold it together. That can come only through structures and systems that encourage convergence and most importantly through a powerful, shared vision, that helps to achieve a degree of uniformity in attitudes and behaviour. Without turning employees into the sort of automatons found in Fritz Lang's *Metropolis*, the organisation has to try to build a set of values that creates consistency. This is the problem of variability of performance that service industries all have to confront in their relationships with consumers. For the corporate brand, variability has to be managed. In his introduction to the RSA *Tomorrow's Company* study (1995), Sir Anthony Cleaver, notes:

> Far too many companies are nowhere near as good as they like to believe, and far too few can support their claims with progress measured and reviewed at board level. I believe this is fundamentally a leadership issue . . . Leadership that has the courage to put across a consistent message which is relevant to all stakeholders – giving the

same vision for the company to shareholder and employee, to investor and supplier, to customer and to the community at large.

The sort of vision that Cleaver is referring to is not the banality of most corporate mission statements, but a true and heartfelt belief that is fundamental to the organisation and steers everything it says and does. To achieve this takes courage, because a vision often flies in the face of accepted norms. Visions that tend towards a middle of the road view are unlikely to engender the sort of devotion needed to coalesce the organisation. The Italian writer, Umberto Eco, has noted that in Italian politics, Socialist, Communist and Christian Democrat arguments become more similar the broader the audience. Corporate visions in their desire not to offend anyone or exclude any opportunity all too often achieve a similar effect. Contrast this with the distinct and impassioned beliefs that steered the development of the British housewares retailer, Habitat, founded in 1964 by Terence Conran. For 25 years, his desire to make things accessible, derived from his socialist, egalitarian education, drove the company. His vision permeated everything Habitat did and inspired the people who worked there:

> His [Conran's] aim was always to deliver to the customer his view of what was right. He would never sell something he didn't think was good, and largely he sold what he personally liked. There was a sincerity and honesty in this that most of the staff wholeheartedly shared . . . Employees quickly got to understand his ideas on products and presentation and, because they were appealingly humanistic, adopted them as their own.[9]

Responsibility

In addition to interacting effectively with all its audiences and balancing their often countervailing needs, the corporate brand also has a broader social responsibility, an ethical imperative. Some organisations such as The Body Shop and Ben and Jerry's Homemade Ice Cream compete in part on their ethical stance towards the environment and employment. Consumers, investors and suppliers who believe in these companies' ethics are not only buying products, but a set of values. Jon Entine, writing in *Dollars and Sense* notes that some of the supposedly ethical stances of companies are more to do with 1960s' liberal ideas of right and wrong, rather than more fundamental truths:

> At best, the relatively small number of consumers with a high tolerance for high priced goods – most of the products [green] in question command a heafty premium over ordinary brands – play a modest role in raising awareness of social problems. (And even so, it's just a prosperous sliver of baby boomers affected.) At worst, cause-related marketing, as it is called, is little more than baby-boom agitprop, masking serious ethical lapses.[10]

Whatever the position of the green marketers, ethics is an issue that confronts all companies. A company does not exist independently of the society within which it operates. It relies on the goodwill of the people who work for it, the local communities within which it is located, the governments that determine legislation and the consumers who buy its products. Support from these groups is not automatic, it requires approval of their activities. As George Bull, Chief Executive, Grand Metropolitan, puts it:[11]

> Increasingly business people are recognising that their prosperity is directly linked to the prosperity of the whole community. The community is the source of customers, employees, their suppliers, and with the wider spread of share ownership, their investors.

Ethics is not a short-term option, but a long-term necessity. More companies now realise this and have clearly stated ethical positions. This is a sensible business stance, not least because the pressures from consumers and legislators have determined that companies that do not abide by the rules that society defines will be punished either through the withdrawal of their consumer franchise or through fines. As an example of this, human rights protests in Burma against the military dictatorship has led to withdrawals from the country by Heineken, Carlsberg, Levi Strauss, Reebok and Pepsi-Cola. The chairman of Heineken was quoted as saying:[12]

> the public opinion and issues surrounding this market have changed to a degree that could have an adverse effect on our brand and corporate reputation.

The glare of publicity that accompanies misdemeanours and miscalculations is extremely damaging. It is all too easy for a company that has a narrow focus on its shareholders and meeting their needs to forget that it has wider responsibilities. As E. F. Schumacher argued in his influential book, *Small is Beautiful – A Study of Economics as if People Mattered* (1974),

What is the meaning of democracy, freedom, human dignity, standard of living, self realisation, fulfilment? Is it a matter of goods, or of people? Of course it is a matter of people.

Businesses are operated by people for people in the context of the society within which we all live. For some organisations, this has been a function of their religious heritage, such as the Quaker companies, Cadbury's and Rowntree's while for others it is derived from a founder's belief, such as the British retailer, The John Lewis Partnership or the American department store chain, Nordstrom. To be credible an ethical position has to be a fundamental part of an organisation's make-up. Aristotle believed that ethical behaviour was the result of habituation. Acting ethically should become automatic and pleasurable, if it is learned and repeated. This implies that business ethics cannot simply be a veneer that in difficult times is stripped away in the pursuit of short-term gain. It must be an inherent part of the company's being.

Summary

A corporate brand is more than just the outward manifestation of an organisation – its name, logo, visual presentation. Rather it is the core of values that defines it. The communication of those values is of course an important part of what an organisation is, for as this chapter has shown, knowledge is often partial. The company that can communicate effectively helps ensure that its various audiences know what it does and what it stands for. It can and should achieve this through understanding the perspectives of its various stakeholders and then building relationships with them that benefit both parties. The important thing to recognise is that communications cannot be based on myth or wishful thinking. Communications must be based on substance. If they are not, inconsistency creeps in and confusion follows shortly thereafter. Employees, for example, can all too easily contradict what is being said in advertising; the reality then fails to match the image. What defines the corporation, in comparison to the brand, is the degree of complexity. It is larger, more diverse and has several audiences that it must interact with. The corporate brand must be able to meet the needs of the often competing claims of its stakeholders. To achieve that it must have clarity of vision, of values and of leadership.

2 The Corporate Environment

Having looked at the core attributes of the corporate brand, it is important to assess its business value. What is it that has changed in the attitudes of people and the activity of society that has made corporate branding so important? This chapter will explore the changes that have determined the *Zeitgeist* of the late 1990s and their impact on the corporate brand. In 1990, the cultural commentator, Peter York believed the spirit of the decade would be one of default – 'a great lack of confident Eightiesness'. By mid-decade York could say,

> And now we are at mid-decade and some real Nineties trends have been developing – many from Eighties roots. Information Technology changing the world of work forever; the real crisis of capitalism following the fall of communism; the melting of civic certainties and the institutions that symbolised them.[1]

York's prognosis is only part of the story.

The triumph of capitalism

With the failure of communism, capitalism has come to be seen to be the only viable model for a modern economy. It has succeeded primarily because it has outlasted its competitors. Communism, as it was expressed in the USSR and Eastern Europe, essentially came apart because its corruption of Marxist principles made the role of the state increasingly untenable without iron fisted rule – something that became difficult to sustain within a global economy with its rapid spread of ideas and information. Eastern bloc communism was destroyed by its own inconsistencies, rather than defeated by capitalism. Nonetheless capitalism no longer has any real rivals: the pre-eminence of the market – where willing buyer meets willing seller for the rational exchange of goods –

seems to be unquestioned. Western governments may laud this fact, but as a result politicians will find their ability to influence events increasingly constrained. There were several examples of this during the 1992 exchange rate mechanism (ERM) crisis, when some EC governments tried to support their currencies to keep them within the pre-agreed exchange rate bands. Just before dropping out of the mechanism with the rate of the pound falling dramatically, the then Prime Minister, John Major, was confident that, 'there will be no devaluation, no realignment of sterling'. The lesson to be learned, apart from treating the pronouncements of politicians with scepticism, is that with the globalisation of business, individual governments often do not have the power to run counter to market forces.

The scope of government has therefore become more limited and in the absence of alternative ideologies, politics has converged towards a centrist position which stresses individualism as its core credo. If governments lack influence in the economic arena, do they enjoy any greater role in social issues? Probably not. Governments in many countries are reducing their involvement in society and seem either unable or unwilling to influence such movements as communitarianism – essentially the idea that community institutions that encourage moral behaviour need to be nurtured. Indeed the American communitarian philosopher Amitai Etzioni has argued against government interference, saying that 'the best way to minimise the role of the state, especially its policy role, is to enhance the community and its moral voice'.

Etzioni is not alone in this stance which has seen politics become marginalised in its influence and legitimacy. Research by Gallup and the Henley Centre for Forecasting shows that the British public's confidence in Parliament has dropped dramatically, from 54% in 1983 to just 9% in 1995 (Figure 2.1). This research is supported by work done by MORI, which shows that only 11% of people trust what government ministers have to say. Nor is Britain an isolated case. In the USA, non-politicians, such as Ross Perot and William Powell, who either have or have been tempted to run for President, have received considerable support, mainly because they seem to have ideas and integrity. Similarly the acclaim and emotive support given to Nelson Mandela around the world is largely because he is a symbol of integrity and humility. Meanwhile careerist politicians are despised and increasingly leaving politics for other professions:

> voluntary departures from Congress are now reaching historic proportions.[2]

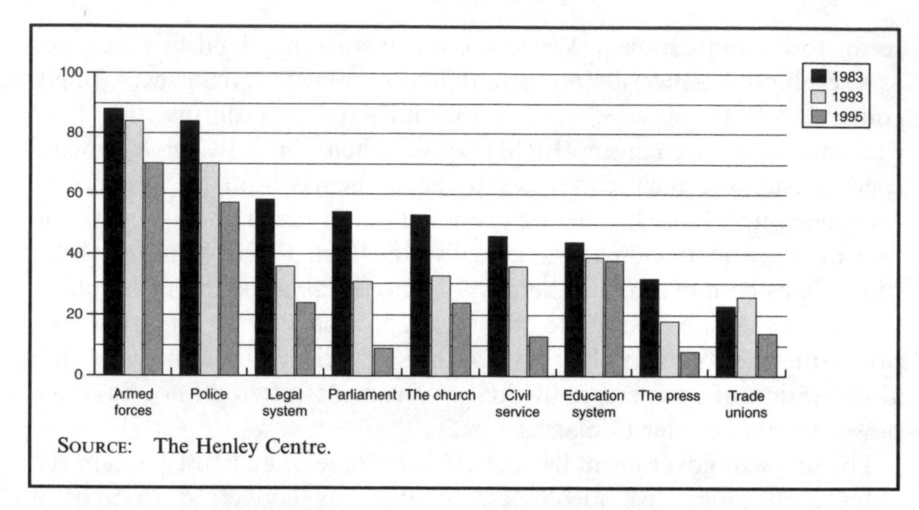

SOURCE: The Henley Centre.

Figure 2.1 Dramatic fall in confidence in institutions: percentage having either 'a great deal' or 'quite a lot' of confidence, 1983–95

If the writer, Kenichi Ohmac is to be believed things are even worse in Japan. Based on the experience of his failed campaign to become governor of Tokyo, he says that government has become powerless to deal with economic problems because it is paralysed by self-serving collusion between producer lobbies, pork-barrel politicians and a bloated bureaucracy dedicated to perpetuating itself.[3]

What, then, will fill the vacuum left by 'the end of politics? Partly it will be taken up by whatever people see as the big issues, such as the environment and morality: just as traditional parties have declined in strength, so pressure groups often built around single issues, such as gun control and abortion, have increased. Partly it can and should be taken up by business. Companies, with their ability to generate wealth and to provide meaning for individuals, in what Hegel described as their 'desire for recognition', are central to our lives. Within a capitalist framework, this provides an opportunity – and a responsibility – for business to be the generator of new ideas, to fill the vacuum left by politics. Generally people are not looking to business or anyone else for radical solutions to their problems, but for companies to remain relevant they will have to question their existing beliefs and look for new ways to meet the needs of society. There will be an onus on companies to communicate and interact with people; to define themselves in terms of brands that are bought by a company's audiences. Consumers will demand high levels of service, shareholders will want more openness and information, local communities will want more involvement and support (research by MORI suggests that 87% of people in Britain believe that large companies have a responsibility to the community) and employees will demand a relationship of reciprocal benefits. While government once presided, fairly exclusively over education and housing, businesses are becoming more involved with both in defining standards and providing support:

> In the past decade, many companies have stepped in where government has failed: in education, in the inner city, in the environment. Environmentally conscious leaders like US Vice President Al Gore ask that companies incorporate so-called externalities into their strategic decisions – that they internalise the clean-up costs of industrial waste and of air, water and land pollution.[4]

The involvement of business in such areas as education has the ring of nineteenth-century paternalism about it: benevolent companies, such as the Victorian department store, Whiteleys and the confectioner, Cadbury's were providing housing, welfare and education for their workers more than 100 years ago. However, now the impetus is not just looking after workers, but a broader awareness that a well educated and functioning society is integral to the effectiveness of business. What has become known as Corporate Community Involvement (CCI) – the planned interaction of businesses with communities in programmes of change – is seeing dramatic growth. The Ethics Resources Centre in Washington, DC has found that 'more than 60% of American companies and almost 50% of European companies now have some type of CCI programmes in place.[5]

Some people see the involvement cynically. MORI asked the question 'Which comes closest to your view of why companies support society and the community?' The responses show that respondents break down into a roughly equal division of positive and negative attitudes:

	(%)
• to cover up anti-social activities	64
• giving very little help and trying to get a lot of benefit	39
• giving real help but expect to benefit from it	46
• genuinely trying to help society and the community	5
• no opinion	6

MORI's findings show that companies still need to do more to convince people of their social probity and to consequently improve their reputation. However, the benefits of such programmes are not confined to a company's image:

> a set of studies commissioned in 1989 and 1992 by IBM and conducted by UCLA's David Lewin examined 156 companies. The results indicate that employee morale was up to three times higher in companies actively involved in their communities.[6]

The alternative to the picture of consensus capitalism is an image of unrestrained profiteering. In some countries, such as Russia, where the rule of law is currently weak, darker economic forces do exist. And indeed, in well developed economies, there will still be companies who are individualistic and self-centred or who deliberately flout accepted behaviour. Although individualism is not necessarily negative, it remains a core credo of Anglo–American business practice – even if the reality of this individualism is disputed by some writers, such as Francis Fukuyama. In many other parts of the world, such as Christian Democratic Northern Europe or Confucian Asia inclusive markets are the norm. In Germany, Scandinavia, Switzerland and Japan the business emphasis is on state involvement, high employment, social cohesion and stakeholder unity. This contrasts directly with the deregulated, litigious, stakeholder conflicting Anglo–American system. However, even within the Anglo–American model the power of the corporation is tempered in two core ways. First, while accepting the limitations of politics, governments still have the power to legislate and police business, in such areas as corporate governance and executive pay. Second, and perhaps more importantly, companies only survive if they are seen as legitimate. Unless they act responsibly and meet the needs of consumers and other stakeholders, support for a business can be withdrawn. Francis Fukuyama argues that without this legitimacy, economic activity would be undermined:

> Virtually all economic activity in the contemporary world is carried out not by individuals but by organisations that require a high degree of social cooperation.[7]

Confident consumers

Going back to how consumers thought and acted in the early 1960s and it is amazing how far we have travelled in terms of confidence and sophistication. In Western Europe and the USA society was transformed in the Cold War years. Consumers, and in particular young consumers, had money to spend on clothes and on their homes. As consumers they needed guidance and support, which was provided in no small part by the emergence of magazines. In the UK, Sunday supplements, such as the *Daily Telegraph* and the *Sunday Times* and style magazines such as *Queen*, *Town* and *Nova* arrived. These publications tried to take the guesswork out of what constituted 'good taste'. In interviewing people about the period, there is a recall of a genuine sense of wonderment at new ideas and products that is notably absent from today's more knowing and cynical consumers. Over the space of 30 years, British consumers discovered wine, foreign holidays, mineral water, curries and pasta. None of these were commonly known to people in the early 1960s. Indeed in 1957, as an April Fool Day's joke, the BBC programme *Panorama* managed to persuade large numbers of people that spaghetti grew on trees. In the early 1970s in France, there were new fashions and ideas – from Mary Quant's mini jupe to the introduction of duvets – and an internationalisation of taste. Young French consumers, guided by the new magazines such as *Maison Marie Claire*, *Maison Francaise* and *Elle Decoration* began to exhibit buying patterns that were distinctively different to those of their parents.

As people have grown more aware of the world around them so they have become more confident as consumers. The Henley Centre for Forecasting has long recognised that consumers can be broadly segmented into confident and less confident consumers, but the important attribute they have detected is that the confident sector is growing. As well as the experience factor, they also note that increasing affluence and 'seeing backstage' (understanding how companies work – which has been abetted by the proliferation of consumer information programmes and magazines) are encouraging people to widen their buying repertoires. No longer can companies rely on loyalty from consumers. People have far less inhibition about exploring new experiences and trying out new brands for different occasions. Whereas, perhaps once consumers would buy only one brand of coffee, now they buy several: one for everyday use, one for indulgence and one for entertaining. Across a large number of product areas the number of people who buy the same brand each time is diminishing rapidly. Henley Centre/Brann research indicates that those people who nearly always buy the same brand in over 50% of markets, constitute only 17% of the population, while the promiscuous, who nearly always buy the same brand in 25% or less of markets, make up 36%.

Much of the promotional activity carried out by companies is designed to address the loyalty problem. Tying people into a particular airline through a frequent traveller programme or a credit card through a bonus points scheme, makes it harder for them to switch brands. Even though an airline may have provided poor service, the consumer has to weigh up the downside in potential lost benefits in changing to another carrier. This is not so much relationship marketing as a form of blackmail. Indeed although, the marketing industry may bracket much of its activity under the label of relationship building, this may be over-stating the case from the consumer perspective. Consumers may have an emotional attitude towards a brand or a company – for example, most graphic designers feel strongly about the Apple Macintosh – but this is not the same as a relationship that we have with family and friends; it is a 'business' relationship based around mutual benefits. The degree of relationship in a purchase is related to its importance. Toothpaste will be relatively unimportant, whereas a car will tend to be important. One has only to look at the cinéma verité-style television programmes on car owners to begin to worry about society's values and people's behaviour. Even if one accepts the term 'relationship' to describe what goes on in the transactions of goods and services, then it is important to recognise that relationships tend not to be instantaneous. The purchase of a product, such as a Mont Blanc pen is only the beginning of a relationship – it is the pleasure of the pen in use that helps cement the marriage. The implication of this is that consumers build relationships not with products *per se*, but more and more with the companies that provide them; with the people who design the product and who service it. This personalisation of business is part of the process of growing sophistication: consumers are more aware of the people behind the products they consume. As a consequence well regarded corporate brands are able to deliver products with ready-made goodwill. Research conducted by advertising agency, FCB during 1995, demonstrated that Virgin has this in volume:

> One company throughout the research emerged as the champion of the 90s consumer. 'I would expect anything that Richard Branson's Virgin provides to be excellent value for money and to put the consumer first', was one comment from the study. Few consumers resent Branson his millions and a number asked when he would be opening up his own supermarket chain.[8]

Trust

With consumer confidence also comes cynicism. Consumers do not necessarily believe what companies tell them about themselves or their products. The growing distrust of institutions and in particular central government is borne out of us knowing more than ever before about the realities of what goes on and the accumulated evidence of broken promises. Raoul Pinnell, Head of Marketing at NatWest UK says: 'in all categories of public and commercial life, trust has fallen. I think that's part of a more open information society.' Companies who fail to deliver quality products or services are regarded poorly. The only way for an organisation to create trust is through meeting people's expectations of honesty and openness. This is the basis of the phenomenal success of the retailer, Marks and Spencer – albeit this has been tarnished by allegations of plagiarism and mis-labelling. Its products are of consistently high quality, the service is exemplary and the no quibble returns policy – in spite of evidence of abuse by some consumers – is studiously adhered to. The company can stretch its brand name to fit financial products with seeming ease – simply because consumers trust Marks and Spencer. Similarly in Japan, trust is central to the web of relationships that companies have with their stakeholders. Much of the success of Japanese business has been attributed by some analysts to the fact that consumers trust companies and their products – in most cases justifiably. In Europe, the absence of trust is the norm. However, there do seem to be variations. Francis Fukuyama in his book, *Trust: The Social Virtues and the Creation of Prosperity* (1995) notes that Germany is a high trust society, largely because its Protestant culture has encouraged the development of intermediate institutions between the family and the state. In contrast, both France and Italy are low trust societies, where faith in non-familial relationships is limited. However, Fukuyama does note that within Italy the basis of trust varies between the North, Central and South regions. This suggests that although societies have long-established and entrenched levels of trust based on cultural values and the performance of institutions, trust in companies has to be earned by positive experience and increasingly by the people and the service behind the brand.

In contrast to the performance of Marks and Spencer, the UK financial sector is generally poor at building trust. Research by MORI into the favourability ratings of companies tends to rank financial retailers at the bottom of the league. A 1995 survey into the sector, sponsored by AT&T, showed that 'only 37% of companies have a team dedicated to customer service and fewer than half have any budget earmarked for developing long-term customer relationships'. The reasons for this are varied. It is not that banks are unaware of the issues – both qualitative and quantitative research demonstrates that senior managers are aware of the problems and opportunities. And some have acted upon it. First Direct Bank, which is a UK-based telephone banking operation is renowned for the quality of its service and has recorded an 80% satisfaction rating against a 45% average for banks. The intriguing aspect of this is that First Direct records a 59% rating for cash machine satisfaction against 32% for Midland Bank – 27 percentage points difference, yet the two banks use the same machines. It would be hard to find stronger evidence for the power of a corporate image.

Yet overall the historical legacy of banks in particular has proved difficult to shake off: banks still think in terms of accounts not customers. This is borne out by FCB's group discussion research (100 groups during 1995):

> All the groups agreed that the banks behave as though they were doing people a favour rather than offering a service. Many thought that instead of there being a service ethic, the old traditions of money lending prevailed.[9]

Intriguingly, the low status of banks in the UK seems to be replicated in the USA, but not in Germany. Brent Keltner of the Rand Corporation, who interviewed more than 60 bank executives before publishing his findings in the *California Management Review*, discovered that one of the core difference between the two countries was in their attitude towards customers. American banks, he argues, are largely focused on acquiring new customers, often through discounts and incentives. In contrast, German banks are much more concerned with building relationships with their existing customers. To this end they invest heavily in training – two to three times as much as American banks – and encourage personal contact with customers. In the German banking system, each employee has specific responsibility for individual customers. Accordingly, whereas American banks have been losing market share and downsizing, German banks have maintained a stable workforce and market share.

The change that has been taking place in consumer attitudes has been creating more individualistic, more demanding and more confident consumers. People are asking for quality and service. The Henley Centre's Dataculture study (1995) has shown there to be a level of irritation among consumers about the imparting of information to companies (54% of people in a quantitative survey agreed that 'giving personal information to companies is a necessary evil'), but consumers accept it, provided they feel in control and see benefits in the exchange. Increasingly those benefits are in the area of product improvement and more effective after-sales service. The latter in particular can be derived only from a more visible corporate brand that engenders a feeling of trust in the mind of the consumer.

Differentiation and the decline of brands

The problems of differentiation have long been recognised in both products and services. Back in 1980, Michael Porter noted:

> Products have a tendency to become more like commodities over time as buyers become more sophisticated and purchasing tends to be based on better information. Thus there is a natural force reducing product differentiation over time in an industry.[10]

As well as the 'natural force', the acceleration in design and manufacturing processes means that one company's innovations – unless they are protected by patents – can be quickly copied. Even in automotive development where lead times are long, the use of simultaneous engineering and CAD/CAM systems has reduced the speed to market. For example Land Rover, who traditionally used to take 60 months to bring a new product to market, produced the Discovery in 27 months. In services, the difficulties are even more pronounced. A financial services product is formed by a combination of rate of return, longevity and penalties or restrictions. There tends to be nothing proprietary about any of these elements, so that if one company varies its terms, others can easily follow. In Britain in the 1980s when building societies began to introduce extra interest accounts, products were introduced and copied by their competitors within the space of a few weeks – the time it took to produce the literature and advertising. When a building society did something genuinely new, there would be a very short window of opportunity to generate additional funds, but the overall long-term difference, and the one which determined consumer behaviour, was the distinctive image of each society, nurtured by advertising and the branches.

In consumer goods, brands need to maintain their point of difference to survive. If the consumer fails to perceive a relevant and distinctive appeal in a brand, then they will purchase a less expensive alternative. The dominance of the UK retailers over brands has been well documented and has been the result of consumer trust in the retailers' offering. In the early 1980s, most retail own-brands were discount alternatives to manufacturers brands. They were certainly cheaper, but most were also poorer quality. This was reflected in the approach to packaging, which was minimalist and designed to emphasise the functionality and value of the product. This 'no-frills offer' began to be replaced as the decade wore on by own-brand alternatives that offered comparable quality, but at cheaper prices. Spearheaded, by the UK supermarket, J Sainsbury, under the banner of 'good food costs less at Sainsbury' retailers began acting like brands, producing advertising that emphasised product quality. The process has now reached its logical conclusion with the introduction of Sainsbury branded products, such as its washing powder, Novon. Now 55% of Sainsbury products are own-label. Why should consumers buy manufacturers' brands? The answer is that manufacturers can point to real points of difference in product performance that extend consumer choice or in those long-term attributes that reassure consumers. As with service, the former is difficult to maintain for any length of time. Provided the industry sector is attractive in terms of potential returns, innovators will quickly find imitators. This is as true for cars as for crisps. Just as the innovation of the people carrier, the Renault Espace, was copied by Japanese and European manufacturers, so Phileas Fogg, which created the adult snacks market in the UK, now faces an overcrowded marketplace.

Nonetheless well-positioned brands still manage to survive and grow. Absolut Vodka for example has been a success throughout the world, not because it is better than other products – Vodka is essentially a commodity product – but because an image of fashionability and sophistication has been maintained by a unique bottle shape and a long-running advertising campaign. Nonetheless, the brand needs to be supported by high levels of advertising and product innovation if it is to maintain its leadership. What would undermine its status would be if fashionability and sophistication ceased to be so important in the vodka market, or if a competitor found a more appealing positioning. One has only to look at the meteoric rise of the Mexican beer, Sol, and its subsequent decline to see the danger of a fashion-based positioning. Whereas once a slice of lime in a beer bottle was the height of trendiness, it is now the opposite. Even the mighty Coca-Cola, once rated by Interbrand as the number 1 brand in the world – before being superseded by McDonald's – and eulogised as 'the quintessential international brand . . . a textbook case of meticulous brand management and development over more than a century',[11] is under threat from new market entrants such as Virgin and look-alike own labels. Although internationally Coca-Cola continues to penetrate new markets, in Britain it has seen both a fall in its market share and a reduction in its premium price.

In many instances the traditional brand is being undermined because of the difficulty of maintaining technical differentiation that matters and because, as we saw in the previous section, consumers are more confident and willing to experiment. Consumers no longer need the reassurance of a brand name to the same degree. What provides the differentiation in both services and products is the corporate brand. The added ingredients of a powerful corporate image and service is the key to relevant differentiation. These are the points of difference that matter to consumers. According to Opinion Research Corp., 9 out of 10 consumers report that when choosing between products that are similar in quality and price, the reputation of the company determines which product or service is bought.[12] It is also worth noting in this context that the rationale for most corporate advertising is not primarily attracting investors nor communicating with the business community, but overwhelmingly increasing awareness of the company among consumers.

Technology and communications

In 1965, Dr Gordon Moore predicted that the number of transistors that could be put on a chip would double every year. In 1975, he amended the prediction to doubling every two years. What has become known as Moore's Law also states that the increase in power is achieved without any rise in production costs. Therefore, during the last 40 years the cost of a transistor has dropped ten million-fold.[13] Although Moore, co-founder and chairman of the world's largest chip company, Intel, now believes that the rate of growth will slow because of the cost of building the increasingly complex factories that manufacture chips, others think that a combination of government support, new chip technology and manufacturing alliances will sustain Moore's Law.

Peter Cochrane of BT, who is a technological optimist, predicts that 'in ten years we might expect to see computers $10^3\times$ more powerful than those of today'. Optical fibre, which already transports 65% of telephone calls world-wide, can transport the entire contents of 1000 human minds on just ten strands.[14] Whatever its rate of growth, the increase in computer power is inexorable and its potential takes us into a world, previously imagined by science fiction writers and film-makers. The dark future portrayed in such films as *Blade Runner* (1981) and *The Terminator* (1984) where robots have started to challenge man's pre-eminence, will hopefully not be our lot, but if forecasts are correct, in 30 years computers will be $10^9\times$ more powerful: 'machines of such power and capability will evolve human characteristics of adaptability, intelligence and personality.[15]

What are the implications of this technological change? Companies will be able to produce more individualised products, uniquely tailored to our needs and to communicate directly with customers through ever more advanced databases, delivered either through traditional methods, such as mailing but increasingly, as we are already seeing, direct from computer to computer. The extension of product choice through adaptability will occur in a number of ways:

- As mentioned in Chapter 1, in financial services retailers will be able to offer a large variety of products through variations in interest rates and payback terms. This simply requires the computer resources to manage the products and employee knowledge to sell them. Increasingly the latter may be taken over by computers that will offer best advice based on the inputs received.
- In manufactured products, flexible production processes, which already allow such companies as Swatch to produce very short runs of different designs, will be applied to more and more products. The benefit to consumers is in increased individualism and product relevance. However, there do seem limits to this. In some areas research has shown that consumers do not want more choice, especially when the products on offer are very similar. For example, it is questionable whether consumers benefit from having to choose between 15 different variants of washing powder, such as colour wash, standard, biological, non-biological and low temperature. However this is as nothing compared to the choice in yoghourts: 312 new variants were launched in UK supermarkets in 1994 alone. The extension of choice must enhance people's lives. In some product areas the range of products is bewildering and confusing rather than beneficial.
- The most valid form of choice enhancement is when the customer is defining the product. Again computerisation will accelerate this process. Manufacturers already do this by producing items to order, such as hand-made suits and furniture systems. This is akin to craft-based production and relies upon either making items from scratch or adapting from a kit of parts. Levi's now offer this service from their own retail outlets. Customers can design their own jeans shape on a computer and have their own one-off cuts. The information is recorded on an EAN code (bar code) and can be recalled anytime the customer wants a new pair of jeans.

  Sometimes, as with car customisation, the adaptation of form and function is undertaken by the user. The Advanced Photo System jointly developed by Kodak, Canon, Fuji, Minolta and Nikon allows the customer to choose between three different frame formats and three different output variants (CD, prints, slides). An extension of this are products with learning capability. A new prototype infra-red remote controller from Polaroid, not only has the capacity to work with all of Polaroid's projectors and presentation devices, its smart chip allows it to learn the codes for all future products. Some products, such as fountain pen nibs or orthopaedic chairs, are designed to adapt through use to the individual's ergonomic requirements.

The key to these various methods of tailoring products is in the knowledge the company has of its individual customer needs and in having sufficiently flexible manufacturing processes to meet them. Without the former the whole concept fails. Interaction drives customisation: the manufacturer and the consumer need to learn from each other.

- The process by which learning takes place is communication. In small-scale organisations this can be face to face, but in larger organisations other means have to be found. Traditionally most communications were mass-market in their orientation and one-way in their flow. Increasingly communications are tailored to smaller segments or are individualised and encourage dialogue. At the broadest level, print production technology allows for the development of carefully targeted magazines that would have been uneconomic a decade ago. More precisely, the cost of telephone communication has fallen dramatically – a transatlantic call in 1956 cost £2.80 per minute; in 1995 it cost £0.50 – and has enabled companies to market themselves and their products via the phone. This process is not always welcomed by consumers, but the relative cheapness of the telephone also provides individuals with the opportunity to be the initiators of the dialogue. Similarly, the Internet enables people to communicate on a global basis for the exchange of information and the purchase of goods. Although banking and transactions via the Internet are fraught with security problems, companies are advertising and providing information via the World Wide Web in rapidly increasing numbers. As well as consumer audiences, the Internet has very real benefits for professional audiences: company annual report and accounts are being published on the Internet, as are academic and research papers. Companies or individuals seeking information on specific areas of interest can also request information from the global Internet user base.

The core benefit of interactive communication will be control – the ability to determine more precisely what we see, read and respond to. From the corporate viewpoint the benefit will be greater knowledge about customers, but there is also a potential downside. As communications fragment into various methods of direct interaction – mailing, telephone and computer – and more precisely targeted media, it will become harder to achieve a consistent tone to corporate messages. Consistency will occur only if there is a clear understanding of what the corporate brand stands for. This does not suggest that everything should be standardised, rather that the message should be personalised within a consistent framework. The potential for disharmony, especially as most organisations are structured vertically by communication discipline and audience is considerable. Equally, if consistency can be achieved, the benefits of economies of communication are significant.

Globalisation

At one level, globalisation is a non-issue. It is so entrenched in management thinking and practice as to be beyond debate. All the arguments that have been defined in the previous sections of this chapter apply equally to international situations as they do to national ones. Or do they? In favour of the universal approach are a number of factors and proselytisers. Kenichi Ohmae argues that

> the pressure for globalisation is driven not so much by diversification or competition, as by the needs and preference of customers. Their needs have globalised, and the fixed costs of meeting them have soared. That is why we must globalise.[16]

Similarly Francis Fukuyama states that although cultural differentiation will remain important,

> increased global competition has forced companies across cultural boundaries to try to adopt 'best practice' techniques like lean manufacturing from whatever source they come. The worldwide recession of the 1990s has put great pressure on Japanese and German companies to scale back their culturally distinctive and paternalistic labor policies in favor of a more liberal model. The modern communications revolution abets this convergence by facilitating economic globalization and by propagating the spread of ideas at enormous speed.[17]

There are indeed strong global drivers. Across the developed and developing world, people are acting in similar ways. Within Europe, consumption of certain products is determined not by nationality but by lifestyle. Within telecoms, for example, the defining characteristic of heavy users is not nationality, but ownership of a mobile phone. In Asia, excluding Japan, it is estimated that there are 250 million brand-conscious consumers,[18] who have similar attitudes and behaviour patterns. This convergence of behaviour has several sources. The demographics across the developed world are very similar: an ageing profile, an increase in single-occupant households (to 25.9% of all households in the UK and 33.6% in Germany in 1991)[19] and a static or declining population. Second global products and advertising help to ensure that people are aware of the same things and able to buy the same things everywhere in the developed world. Third global media and film, in its predominantly American form, helps to define more universal lifestyles. It is notable that one of the things that worries the French establishment is the loss of French identity and the dominance of American culture. In the Uruguay round of the GATT (General Agreement on Trade and Tariffs) one of the key sticking points was the dominance of American film. America, then, has become the defining world culture: its values and ideas predominate. Similarly in business, Japan has emerged as the progenitor of global marketing and manufacturing thinking. The accessibility of information in both spheres means that good ideas are widely copied, often without regard to cultural dissimilarities. Japanese manufacturing methods in the UK have often been imported wholesale without regard to indigenous working practices:

> Nissan went out of its way to fuse cultures when it arrived; Toyota imported its Japanese ways unchanged, and is seen by British managers as the more frustrating to work for . . . Where a Western firm will try to adapt (to other cultures), the Japanese – with the odd exception such as Nissan – will rarely do so.[20]

Similarly British politicians of both left and right are keen to learn from and copy the economic success of East Asian economies: 'nations that succeed in future will be those that are porous to new ideas from wherever they may come'.[21] However, the idea that the practices of one country can simply be applied to another without adaptation is worrying.

> . . . it is foolish to think there any simple lessons to be learnt from Asia. We know it is difficult enough to copy from the United States or Germany; learning from Taiwan or South Korea is a far trickier

> process. What may work in one culture may prove quite alien in another.[22]

It is possible to sell one brand world-wide: Coca-Cola, McDonald's, Levi's, Sony have shown us how it can be done. The mobility of people and the pervasiveness of media stimulates awareness of these brands. (For example, McDonald's achieves a global awareness figure of 84%.) This suggests the importance of creating systems and values that ensure consistency of performance and communication whatever the vagaries of the local market – Coca-Cola has been built on this premise. However, running counter to the universal approach to global markets are products that suggest an alternative viewpoint. At the simplest level there are cultural differences that require products to be tailored to local markets; the Japanese do not like the smell of leather car seats, the French buy saucepans without lids and the British like strong mustard. At a deeper level we can observe more fundamental differences. It may be true that there are 250 million middle-class consumers in Asia, but equally throughout the world there are a huge number of people effectively disenfranchised from consumerism. Coca-Cola may be a global brand, but 1 billion people lack access to clean water. Sony may be recognised globally, but 2 billion people lack electricity. The American academic Samuel Huntington pointed out, in a seminal article in the journal *Foreign Affairs*, that the 8 civilisations of the world – Western, Confucian, Japanese, Islamic, Hindu, Slavic–Orthodox, Latin American and African – are radically different from each other. He also rejected the idea that as travel increases and communications improve, these differences will become less profound. Rather, as in France, they will become more intense as people struggle to retain their cultural identity. Whereas Fukuyama asserts the world-wide dominance of liberal democracy and the end of history, Huntington stresses the limited nature of western values and their decline,

> Modernisation is often associated with the idea of a single, universal civilisation. What people usually mean by universal civilisation refers to the assumptions and values held by *most* people in the west and by *some* people in other civilisations . . . As western power recedes, so too does the appeal of western values and culture – much of the world is becoming more modern and less western.[23]

If Huntington is right, then the differences between cultural groups may dictate that it will become increasingly difficult to sell truly global brands.

Brands may have to become more adaptive, in terms both of their performance and their presentation to overcome newly heightened cultural barriers. Current assumptions about American cultural hegemony may have to be re-thought. The American economy may currently be more than twice the size of China, but by 2020 the World Bank estimates that China will have easily outstripped America. What will be the implications of this for the global corporate brand? It will not undermine the need to plan and market on a global basis, indeed, for the corporate brands of the West, understanding the economies and cultures of the East will be vital to their success. However, if cultural identities do become more pronounced – and the actions of the Chinese will be fundamental to this – then the corporate brand will have to work harder at becoming an 'insider' in all the cultures it operates in. This will necessitate greater autonomy for each cultural sphere. At present, most of the signs support the notion of increasing globalisation, but there are some factors which suggest this shouldn't be taken for granted. For now, liberal democracy is the dominant global political system, but in the future, Confucian autocracy could be the defining belief.

Summary

This chapter has shown some of the key ways in which changes in society and the business environment are impacting on companies and the way in which they represent themselves. It seems clear that there is a requirement for companies to act legitimately. Consumers and other audiences simply will not tolerate a company that fails to meet its obligations. This is a consequence of ever more confident and questioning stakeholders. Nor is this a peculiarly British phenomenon. As markets become increasingly globalised, so do the issues that define companies' spheres of interest.

Companies need to act as brands that meet the needs of consumers, investors, legislators and employees. This will not always be easy as these various needs will sometimes be in direct opposition to one another. It will be achievable only if a company is united around some core values that allow it to reconcile these opposing interests. A company needs to create an atmosphere of trust through communication and dialogue. New technology has created the means to do this with a large volume of people. Now all that is lacking is the will. Those companies that seize the opportunity to build closer relationships; to value customers and to satisfy their needs, will reap the reward of loyalty (Figure 2.2).

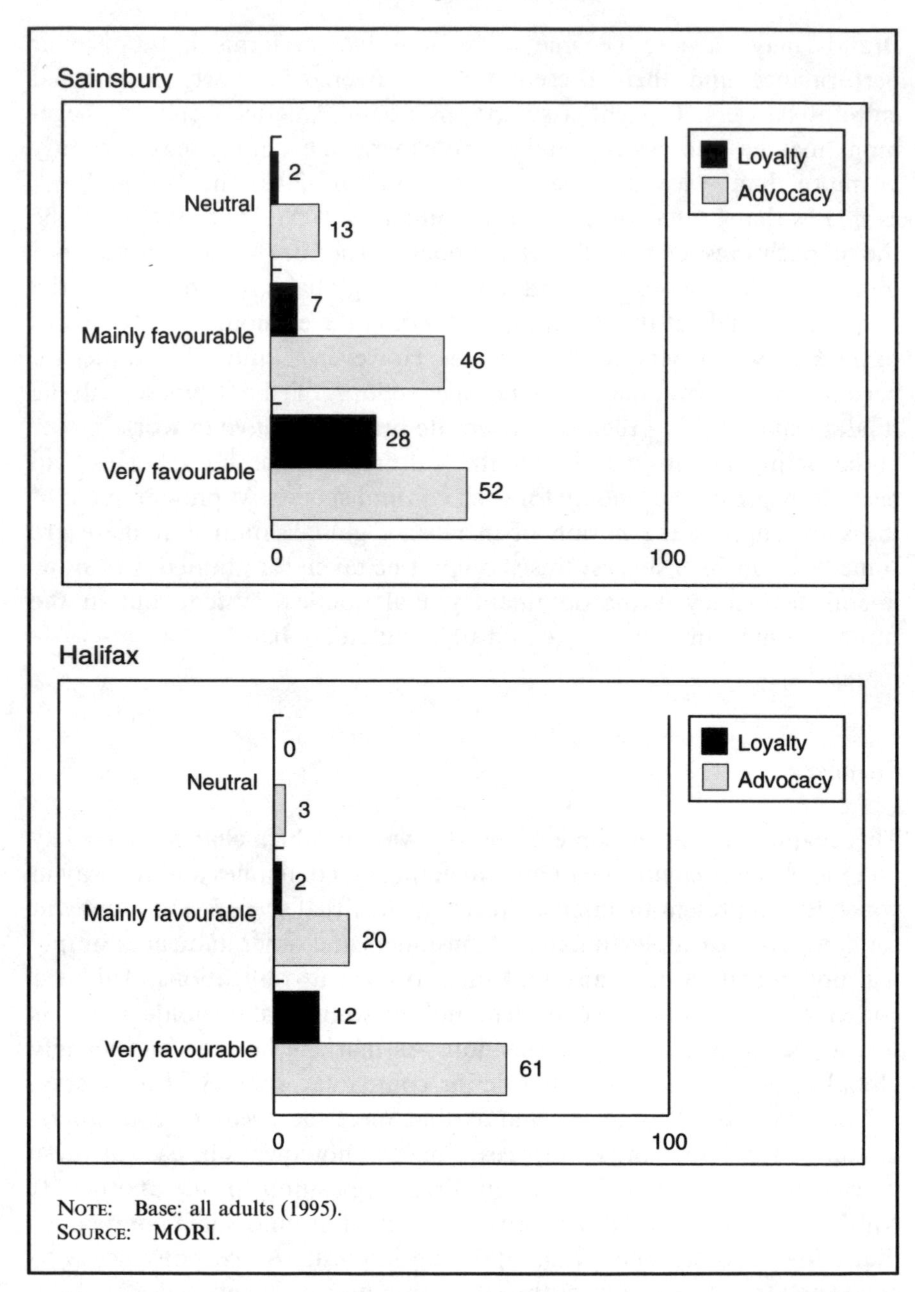

NOTE: Base: all adults (1995).
SOURCE: MORI.

Figure 2.2 Loyalty, advocacy and favourability: Sainsbury and Halifax[24]

3 Corporate Strategy and the Corporate Brand

'Strategy' is concerned with positioning a company so that it can meet its long-term objectives. It should always be unique to an organisation and built on an analysis of competencies and market opportunities/threats. The question is: how do we define an organisation's competencies and how do we know if they matter to stakeholders? In manufacturing, often the competencies are technological, such as Sony's skills in miniaturisation or Bausch & Lomb's (the makers of Ray-Ban sunglasses) optics expertise. In services the competencies are derived from corporate culture, operating systems and human resources policies. For example, the American department store group, Nordstrom, excels at service provision primarily because of its humanistic corporate culture and its emphasis on people quality. However the competency on its own can be negated if the product or service delivery is not relevant to consumer needs. Therefore although competency analysis tends to encourage companies to look inward at themselves and ask what are we good at, in reality they should think more about the customer benefits they are good at meeting. Nordstom's service excellence would not be effective if it resulted in excessively high prices that consumers were unwilling to pay. The other key success factor is the precision with which the organisation's competence is defined. It could be argued that the failure of Apple to dominate the personal computer industry, in spite of its invention of the market and its on-going technological superiority, has been due to an imprecise understanding of its skills. Apple developed the personal computer business by developing both hardware and software. However, its real ability was in making computerisation accessible:

> In naming his new company Apple, Steve Jobs demystified computers and computing. He recognised that the future of his new business lay not with the fanatical, knowledgeable computer expert, but with the man and woman in the street. He had to appeal to an audience which knew nothing about computers and did not wish to know anything.[1]

The company's problems have resulted from trying to maintain its hardware/software base. Hardware has become more and more of a commodity market, which requires manufacturing and logistical skills.

By and large consumers are not motivated by the product form – computers are largely a box with a keyboard – whereas the ease of use of the software is a key differentiator. In retrospect, Apple would have benefited from licensing the manufacturing – as JVC did successfully with its VHS video format – and concentrated on selling its operating systems and its software. As the famous '1984' advertisement demonstrated, Apple saw its competitor as IBM, whereas the real emerging power was Microsoft, to whom Apple mistakenly sold its windows-based software. Now the problem that Apple loyalists face is that there is limited Apple Macintosh software available and the PC-based Microsoft alternative 'Windows' product offers similar performance. Apple has now effectively given up the battle to dominate its industry to Microsoft and instead has decided to concentrate its efforts on becoming a focused product aimed at markets, such as design, where it possesses a competitive advantage.

The notion of achieving competitive advantage for a corporate brand is itself derived from the widely adopted analytical model developed by Michael Porter, whose ideas about strategic clarity have been adopted by companies all around the globe. The core of Porter's ideas is a strategy model which along one axis has competitive advantage and along the other competitive scope (Figure 3.1). The essence of his argument is that companies must choose between being different and being the lowest cost producer in a particular industry. His view is that being stuck in the middle is the route to failure – companies must choose to be one or the other. In the Apple example the company started out as being in the differentiated box, but now it is moving into differentiation focus. As noted already, part of its problem is that as the hardware industry has commoditised it is the lowest cost producer box that is the target of the successful manufacturer. Although Porter's idea has had reasonable longevity as a management theory revisionism now seems to have set in. The economist, John Kay, points out that when you look at return on investment by strategic position, being stuck in the middle tends to produce better returns than being a low cost producer (Figure 3.2). Whether this really undermines Porter's views is debatable. Porter would probably argue that it is no good simply being in the low cost quartile, to succeed you have to be *the* lowest cost producer. The second defence of the model is that Porter argues even when a company aims for differentiation, it should also do everything it can to reduce its costs, but not at the expense of differentiation. In other words, if a company wants to be differentiated on the basis of the quality of its customer service, it can cut only costs that do not affect that service.

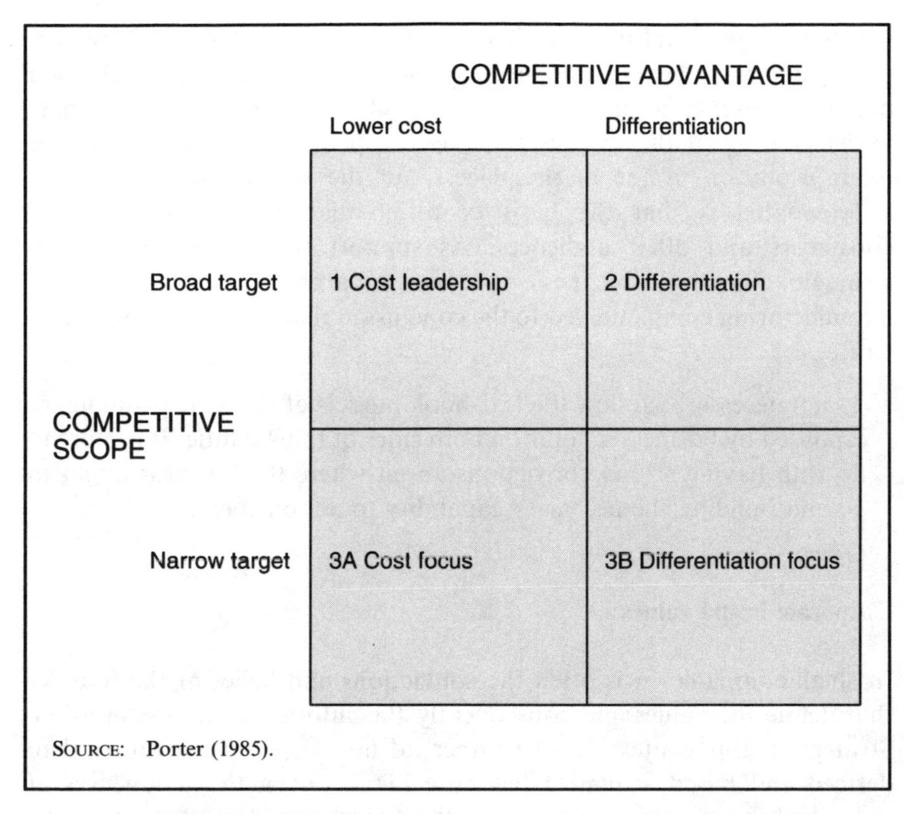

SOURCE: Porter (1985).

Figure 3.1 Competitive advantage and competitive scope

COSTS RELATIVE TO COMPETITORS	QUALITY RELATIVE TO COMPETITORS: Low	Medium	High
Low	11.7	14.2	19.7
Medium	6.8	13.9	17.9
High	3.4	4.8	13.8

SOURCE: J. Kay, *Financial Times* (10 May 1996), p. 17.

Figure 3.2 Return on investment, by strategic position (%)

Whatever the validity of the Porter model, its real value is its emphasis on organisations having a defined and clear direction to help guide their decision making; a direction that should be based on an intimate understanding of the organisation, its competitors, customers and the likely evolution of the marketplace. And the real point about being differentiated is that the basis of differentiation has to matter to consumers and other audiences. As support for the importance of strategic clarity in business success, research among 490 British manufacturing companies led to the conclusion that successful companies strategies

> do not necessarily follow the text-book models of strategic planning, as espoused by business schools on both sides of the Atlantic. It is more to do with having strong convictions about where the business ought to go and building the necessary capability to act on them.[2]

Corporate brand values

In small companies it is often the convictions and belief of the founder that define the values and consequently the culture of the organisation. Strategy in this context can be rather ad hoc; experienced rather than defined and based around a few core ideas. Given the uniqueness of individual experience, the culture will be unique and reinforced by the founding group. Edgar Schein notes:

> the emphasis in this early stage will be on differentiating oneself from the environment and from ofher groups. The group will make its culture explicit, integrate it as much as possible, and teach it firmly to newcomers (or select them for initial compatibility). This process can be clearly seen in rapidly growing young companies. Their self image of how they do things is strongly articulated, explained in detail to newcomers, and re-articulated frequently in ambiguous or critical situations.[3]

The example of Nike

When the sports and fitness brand Nike was founded by a track coach called Bill Bowerman and Phil Knight, a college runner from the University of Oregon, its values were defined by attitudes and circumstance. Nike had two core attributes: a devotion to sporting excellence and an irreverent informality. The commitment to sport came from Knight's background as a runner and in the early days the employees were also sportsmen and women. When Nike set up in the UK in the early 1980s they appointed the long-distance runner, Brendan Foster to run the operation rather than a businessman. The informality was derived from two sources. First, the business itself started informally. Knight ran the company in the early days, while still working full time as an accountant. Second, the company had strong links with the University of Oregon and reflected its atmosphere. When the company grew large enough to have a corporate headquarters, it was designed in the style of a campus. Irreverence and a questioning attitude also prevailed. These were borne out of Knight's beliefs and the way the company was run:

> throughout its first decade and arguably throughout its history, Knight's company was not run from the top down on any level other then production and finance. Knight, instead of administering his company like a president, nodded encouragement from afar as did Bowerman standing high in the stands during a track meeting.[4]

The company's culture was also reflective of the culture of its location,

> Nike Inc., would grow up a lot like Oregon itself, friendly, but intensely private, resolute but flexible . . . Nike didn't have foundations it had roots.[5]

Nike's unique and strong value system drove the company's decision making and communications. The very distinctive advertising that has helped develop the brand has been based on the idea of 'irreverence justified' – the combination of corporate culture and successful products for serious athletes. The irreverence also comes through in the use of Nike's endorsees. Its first star tennis signing in 1973 was the controversial Romanian player, Ilie Nastase, and it has continued to use stars that reflect its stance, such as the footballer Eric Cantona and the basketball player Charles Barkley. One of the interesting aspects of Nike is that it has retained its youthful enthusiasm as it has grown and become more structured. In this respect it is probably atypical, but what David Potter of Psion calls 'corporate memory' – the collective remembrance of events and ideas – is an important factor in ensuring continuity among all organisations:

> People talk about corporate culture, but there are much deeper roots in companies than people normally appreciate. I would go further and say there's more than corporate culture, there's corporate memory or genetics.[6]

Maintaining values

As most organisations develop and evolve, so do their cultures and strategies. The key requirement is to remember and retain those core values that have defined success while adapting to changing conditions. Knowing what to keep and what to change is a difficult balancing act: for example, should Apple Computer in confronting losses and a declining market share discard the laid back, egalitarian, innovative West Coast culture that originally made it successful for a more structured and disciplined approach that perhaps it now needs and that financial audiences want to see, or in so doing will it lose its empowering zeal? In any case, even if Apple management wants to become more disciplined, will it be possible to change such a deeply entrenched culture? Certainly it is easier to evolve cultures rather than change them fundamentally. A company that has always built its strategy around differentiation will find it very difficult to switch to a cost leadership stance, and vice versa. The structures and beliefs that an organisation develops are a major inhibitor to this.

Often the telling point in the evolution of an organisation is when the original founder leaves and the value system has to be maintained without the same personal influence:

> succession processes must therefore be designed to enhance those parts of the culture that provide identity, distinctive competence and protection from anxiety.[7]

The effective communication of 'corporate memory' enables organisations to act intuitively – people know the course of action they should take, because the principles that define management and employee actions are so deeply imbued. One of the best examples of this is Johnson & Johnson. The company has a long-standing reputation built around the quality of its products and its strong and caring beliefs, that is defined in the company's credo (see Box 3.1).

The power of the credo is such that it determined Johnson & Johnson's reaction to seven cases of cyanide poisoning due to tampering with its pain relief drug, Tylenol. After one victim died the company recalled all its products, launched an advertising campaign about the problem and offered a reward for information leading to the arrest of the murderer. The costs of the exercise were enormous, but Johnson & Johnson's sense of social responsibility, which its managers put down to the credo, enabled the company to re-establish the brand after the crisis and to

Box 3.1 The Johnson & Johnson Credo

We believe our first responsibility is to the doctors, nurses and patients, to mothers and all others who use our products and services. In meeting their needs everything we do must be of the highest quality. We must constantly strive to reduce our costs in order to maintain reasonable prices. Customers' orders must be serviced promptly and accurately. Our suppliers and distributors must have an opportunity to make a fair profit.

We are responsible to our employees, the men and women who work with us throughout the world. Everyone must be considered as an individual. We must respect their dignity and recognise their merit. They must have a sense of security in their jobs. Compensation must be fair and adequate, and working conditions clean, orderly and safe. Employees must feel free to make suggestions and complaints. There must be equal opportunity for employment, development and advancement for those qualified. We must provide competent management, and their actions must be just and ethical.

We are responsible to the communities in which we live and work and to the world community as well. We must be good citizens – support good works and charities and bear our fair share of taxes. We must encourage civic improvements and better health and education. We must maintain in good order the property we are privileged to use, protecting the environment and natural resources.

Our final responsibility is to our stockholders. Business must make a sound profit. We must experiment with new ideas. Research must be carried on, innovative programs developed and mistakes paid for. New equipment must be purchased, new facilities provided and new products launched. Reserves must be created to provide for adverse times. When we operate according to these principles, the stockholders should realise a fair return.[8]

maintain its favourable reputation. Compare this to the reluctance of Exxon. Professor Stephen Greyser, of the Harvard Business School, describes the Exxon approach:

> in June 1994, headlines proclaimed 'Jury finds Exxon acted recklessly in Valdez oil spill'. This was another chapter, five years after the start, of a story born in disaster in Alaska's Prince William Sound . . . nurtured in what I consider misconceived apologetic Exxon communications to soften the blow and refurbish its image . . . continued in courtrooms where negligence was a principal theme . . . and still after five years punctuated by negative headlines! The Problem? Not communications . . . but substance. It is Exxon's behaviour that is being judged by the public to have fallen short. Its reputation has slumped.[9]

The fall from grace was even more remarkable given that Exxon was *Fortune* magazine's 6th most admired company in the USA in 1989 – it hasn't figured in the top 10 since the Valdez disaster.

Summary

The corporate brand is concerned with the combination of behaviour and communications that results in the image an organisation has with its stakeholders. The glue that holds these elements together is, as we have seen, the basic assumptions and values of the company. And it is the values that also determine the corporate strategy. Johnson & Johnson's assumptions are radically different from those of Exxon and seemingly better at maintaining a positive reputation. The conundrum then is to question why, if one set of values and a certain strategy seems successful, it isn't universally adopted? One key factor is that individual values are very different – for example, some leaders believe in empowering their employees, while others like to curtail employee freedom. Secondly, organisations have different shared experiences. It is the way that crises or opportunities are handled that creates the core assumptions of an organisation. For example, if Johnson & Johnson were again confronted with the Tylenol problem, they would know from their previous experience the right way to react. Lastly, the ability and willingness to communicate strategy, especially to employees varies enormously and is determined by the value the organisation attaches to communications (this will be discussed further in Chapter 6). A strategy has no value unless it is communicated and acted upon by employees:

> Most corporate strategy statements never actually penetrate the ranks of management to touch the minds of the employees doing the everyday work of a company. Yet they are the people facing customers and clients daily and for good or ill, creating the true image and reputation of the business . . . If your employees don't know what the strategy is, or can't translate it into workable terms, the strategy will simply grind into oblivion somewhere in the offices of senior management.[10]

4 Analysing the Corporate Brand

Having looked at the nature of the corporate brand and the environmental factors that are making it increasingly important to competitive success, this chapter will suggest the means by which we can analyse the brand. Inevitably, the recommended approach is not the one and only universal route and there are other models that are worthy of consideration. However the model detailed below does have the following advantages:

- it links together marketing communications, human resources and products
- it stresses the importance of seeing things from the viewpoint of the organisation's stakeholders
- it recognises the constraining and liberating effects of corporate culture
- it relates the corporate brand's position to the corporate strategy.

The corporate branding model

One of the better known models in the field of strategic corporate identity is that developed by Abratt (1989) and presented in a paper called 'A New Approach to the Corporate Image Management Process.'[1] Abratt argued that there were three aspects to corporate image management: corporate personality, corporate identity and corporate image. Personality encompasses such areas as corporate philosophy, values and strategy which influences the identity, which Abratt sees as concerned with communication objectives and structures. The identity then interfaces with an organisation's various audiences to form an image based on organisational reality. Abratt's model was further developed by an Australian academic, Helen Joyce Stuart, who based her judgement on research into the identity and image of 44 accountancy firms. She found that the separation of corporate identity into its communication aspects and personality/cultural attributes was artificial. She also stated that:

whereas Abratt (1989) includes employees as one of the stakeholder groups that are influenced by corporate image, I consider them to be a special group who are impacted upon by corporate identity, and with a successful marketing program are an effective means of communicating the corporate identity, synergistically with an effective marketing communications strategy. The interface is then defined as the point at which communication of the corporate identity takes place, converting it into a corporate image, or perhaps several corporate images.[2]

Stuart's adaptations of the model are useful, but perhaps because of her focus on corporate image and perhaps also because of her focus on a service industry, the model misses out a key box, which is a key determinant of both identity and image: the products and services provided by an organisation (Figure 4.1). In general terms, in any company where there is a clear association between products and the organisation that produces them – Sony, BMW, Microsoft – those products will define and influence the image of all key audiences. Similarly, in this model, there is a clear link between a company's

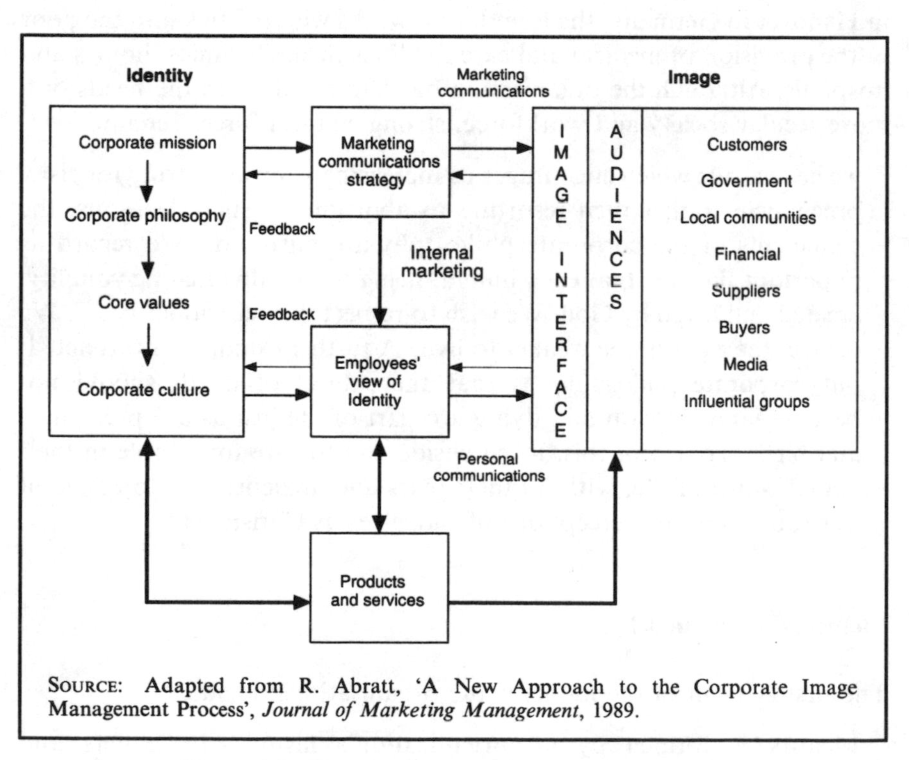

SOURCE: Adapted from R. Abratt, 'A New Approach to the Corporate Image Management Process', *Journal of Marketing Management*, 1989.

Figure 4.1 Integrated approach to communications

products and its identity: the nature of the product influences an organisation's culture and identity, while the identity in turn influences the nature of the product. For example, Psion was originally highly successful as a manufacturer of computer games and was at one point market leader in the UK. However, the leaders of the company, and in particular David Potter, who came from an academic and technology background, were driven by two ideals. One was to produce innovative products and the other was to reach as wide a market as possible. In an interview Potter says:

> we purposely decided to get out of that [computer games] for two reasons. One, because we didn't think that kind of market would endure in that form. Second, was a cultural one: I didn't want to spend my life in computer games and it wasn't in the culture of the people around me. That's why we searched for new areas and ended up in applications software and volume hand held computers.

Another powerful example of the impact of identity on products and services is the religious charitable foundation, Henriettenstiftung. Based in Hanover in Germany, the foundation works with the sick and the poor in the provision of medical and care facilities through clinics, homes and hospitals. Although the organisation has had to adapt to the needs of a more secular society and workforce, strong cultural forces remain:

> we have a rule which encourages us increasingly toward caring for risky pregnancies rather then resorting to abortion. In such decisions, the statements of the corporate philosophy are mirrored: 'We regard as important the idea that each human being is an individual personality, created and loved by God. We wish to respect this individuality . . . We protect the right of the weaker to live.' A further example of this acted-out corporate philosophy is that the subject of death should not become taboo. Death and dying are part of life just as are pregnancy and birth. To accept this, to be beside and to care for people in their varied walks of life, with all their fears and anxieties, is expressive of our roots and our perceptions of ourselves as Christians.[3]

Elements of the model

The first element of the model is the organisational identity:

> Identity is formed by an organisation's history, its beliefs and philosophy, the nature of its technology, its ownership, its people,

> the personality of its leaders, its ethical and cultural values and its strategies. It can be projected or communicated through corporate identity programmes, but identity *per se* is very difficult to change. It is not something cosmetic, but is the core of an organisation's existence.[4]

Each identity is therefore unique and derived from the shared experience of individuals over time. In the previously cited example of the Henriettenstiftung, the identity clearly has a strong religious tradition, which has been evolved to meet the realities of a more secular world. However the evolution has not undermined the essence of the religious thinking.[5]

In any well established organisation, identities tend to be very resistant to change. This is partly because the basic assumptions that guide attitudes and behaviour become unconscious and unquestioned. Collective experience dictates that a certain way of doing things works. For example, an organisation that believes in environmentalism as a core principle will not question whether this is valid every time it has to make a decision – the principle will define the action. In the case of a corporate trauma, the principle can either reinforce behaviour (as in the instance of the Johnson & Johnson Tylenol example on p. 38) or a set of values may have to be reappraised (such as IBM's commitment to full employment in the face of a downturn). To bring this point home, one has only to think of our national cultural assumptions and how they sometimes are rudely awakened when we confront other nationalities.

Marketing communications strategy

The marketing communications strategy should in itself be unique, because it will be based on the values inherent in the identity. The strategy is concerned with meeting the communication objectives of the organisation and defining the roles for the communications media, such as advertising, literature, exhibitions and direct marketing. The core attributes of the marketing communications strategy are:

- it is focused on satisfying (and preferably exceeding) the needs and aspirations of the organisation's various audiences
- it is single-minded
- it is sustained across all media
- it has potential longevity
- it is concerned only with communicating what is deliverable

Broadly, these attributes try to ensure an outward focus on the reality of the marketplace and try to ensure quality and consistency in communications. This is not to suggest that all audiences receive exactly the same message, for if an organisation is to build some form of relationship with its investors, customers and suppliers, communications should be tailored to meet specific interests and needs. However, throughout the range of communications there should be a distinctive and recognisable continuity of tone. Take any well developed brand – Benetton, *The Economist*, Absolut Vodka, Orange, First Direct Bank – and there is enormous consistency of tone in the communications, even when the message and the audience varies. It is possible with all of these brands to cover up the brand name yet achieve instantaneous recognition from the colour (Orange, *The Economist*), shape (Absolut), type (First Direct) and imagery (Benetton).

Employees' view of identity

The employees' view of identity will be determined by the overall culture of the organisation – the assumptions and values of the organisation that are transmitted by the collective attitudes and behaviour – and by the communications process. Of course, there may be more than one culture in an organisation. Indeed it is likely that each business group will have its own ideas of what constitutes 'acceptable behaviour'. For example, within, the food and drinks giant, Grand Metropolitan, each division has a clearly defined identity with its own beliefs and ideas. However, in large companies, the ideal is that in addition to the identities of the business units, there is a clear recognition of, and loyalty to the identity of the parent.

One of the key tasks of communications is to help reinforce the existing culture. Assuming that the culture is part of the reason for a company's success it is vital that the core cultural attributes are maintained. If an organisation's performance is founded on an informal style, such as Nike, then it would be dangerous, if a new chief executive tried to transform it into a deferential bureaucratic company. The opposite is probably even harder to countenance. When Sir Terence Conran, the founder of the UK retailer Habitat, acquired the long-established store group, British Home Stores (BHS), he encountered an entirely alien culture, which proved extremely resistant to change. Habitat's culture was a reflection of Conran's personality: it was informal, energetic and confrontational. No deference was given in meetings and people could be aggressive with each other in putting forward a particular point. In contrast, the defining culture of BHS was formal and deferential. Surnames were used by employees and meetings were not occasions to put across your ideas, rather they were the opportunity to support the ideas of superiors: arguing against one's immediate superior at BHS would be the end of a career. Conran would tell BHS employees to just call him Terence, but it was impossible for them to make the change, and they always persisted in referring to him formally, as 'Sir Terence'.

Products and services

The final element in the communications process are the products and services supplied by an organisation. The nature of the service and product, should be defined by the basic assumptions of the organisation and the resulting strategy. Further it should integrate with the marketing communications and the actions of individuals (in a service company, the people aspect is fundamental to the service delivery). A powerful example of a service organisation that once delivered consistent communications through everything it did was London Transport. Frank Pick, General Manager of London Transport in the 1930s, supported by his chairman Lord Ashfield, set high-minded principles for the organisation, which concerned themselves with contributing, 'their appointed share to the transformation of our urban civilisation into some fine flower of accomplishment'. This vision of transport's central role in society defined the organisational culture, and covered all aspects of the service

> including staff motivation, service quality, communications and design . . . Visual matters were accorded particular attention, with the design of stations, rolling stock, information, promotional material and other items now being regarded as classics individually and as a whole. For Pick, every aspect and detail mattered.[6]

With manufacturers, it is often the physical product that defines our relationship as consumers to the company. The German appliances company, Braun, is typical in this respect. What we perceive to be the truth about Braun is determined by the look, feel and functionality of the products. Our perceptions are in part determined by experience of German products generally, whether they be cars or food mixers: the cultural presumption is that the product will be efficient, well made, simple in its surface design and functional. In German design, 'ornament is crime'. As a manufacturer, Braun was strongly influenced by the principles of the German design school, the Bauhaus. Its logo, unchanged for 40 years, is simple and clear, while the products have long followed the principles of its head designer, Dieter Rams, 'less design is more design'. The founder's son, Erwin Braun, described the company's ethos as follows:

> Our appliances must be silent, unobtrusive servants. They go about their business quietly, always there when you need them, but otherwise discretely unnoticed.

The corporate image

> Corporate image is in the eye of the receiver. An organisation may transmit a message about itself to its employees, its investors, its customers, and all its internal and external audiences. It may indeed wish to convey a particular self image, but it is the reception of the message that is the important factor. The corporate image is simply the picture that an audience has of an organisation through the accumulation of all received messages.[7]

Although the model adopts a logical approach in the flow of information from identity through communications to image, in reality it is better to turn the whole concept around. This makes the audiences the most important element in the process and helps to ensure the organisation is outward facing and focused on meeting the needs and wants of its stakeholders. Unless organisations have a structure or system that encourages them to look outwards, the tendency will be towards introspection. The other important point to note is that communications don't just happen when the organisation decides to launch a corporate advertising campaign, it occurs all the time through the actions of individuals, comments in the media and the consumption of products and services. Therefore an image is not a controllable event, it is an on-going, uncontrollable relationship. The aim for any organisation is to exert as much credible influence over that relationship as possible, so that the corporate image is:

- appropriate to the company
- supportable by the corporate culture
- relevant to the corporate strategy
- clear and consistent

We have already noted in Chapter 1 that people like to rearrange the information they receive so that it is understandable in their own terms. This suggests that it is important for companies to be consistent in their communications – at least as far as is possible within this uncontrollable environment. Consistency gives the organisation its best chance to get its message across. Inconsistent communications tend to lead to confused audiences who either have only a vague idea of the organisation, or a very negative one. The benefits of consistency are clear and evident in some of the powerful corporate brands already cited in this book: Virgin, Marks and Spencer, BMW and Microsoft. Compare the relationship that Marks and Spencer enjoys with its consumers, with Shell (Table 4.1).

Table 4.1 Consumer relationships

	Shell (%)	*M&S* (%)
Advocacy	1	15
Loyalty	17	55
Satisfaction	40	70
Transaction	48	72
Trust	89	97
Awareness	89	97
Ad spend	£5m	Not listed in top 250 advertisers in UK

SOURCE: MORI (1996).

Or Virgin with its peers (see Figure 4.2).

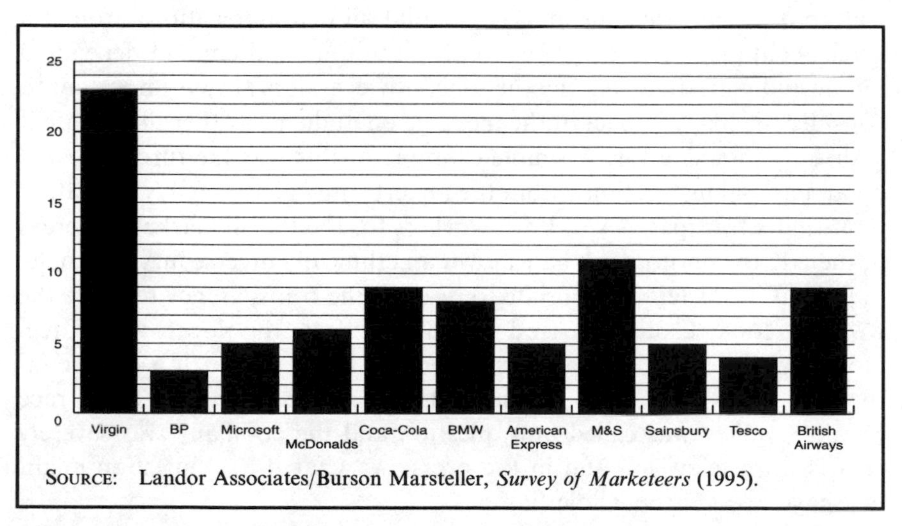

SOURCE: Landor Associates/Burson Marsteller, *Survey of Marketeers* (1995).

Figure 4.2 'Thinking about companies other than your own, which 5 corporate brands do you admire most?'

The interesting aspect of Marks and Spencer's performance is that it has been achieved with virtually no advertising, whereas Shell and others, such as BP (which shows almost identical ratings to Shell) have been big spenders. The image of Marks and Spencer has largely been created through the usage of the stores and the consistency of the product quality, whether it be underwear or food. Similarly, Virgin's youthful enthusiasm and dynamism is carried through the style of all its products, from cola to airlines. In both these instances, the organisational culture is vitally important. It is the power of the shared values and the organisational commitment to a few simple ideas that drives the organisations forward in a cohesive way, so that the actions of employees endorse the quality of the products and services to create a relationship of trust with their consumers. It is notable that both Marks and Spencer and Virgin have been able to enter the financial services market and instantly acquire the sort of trust that most of the industry has always found elusive.

Outside of consumers, there are a whole range of people who take an interest in the activities of an organisation. Government, journalists, local communities, investors, suppliers, buyers and future employees will all take note of what an organisations says and does. And their agendas may be very different from those of consumers. This suggests that messages to these audiences will need to be tailored depending on their information needs, but as we have observed the difficulty in achieving this is that there is often audience overlap: journalists are also consumers. The rational way to deal with this dilemma is to build all communications around a single, credible positioning, but to alter the tone and content depending on the audience. In amending the tone, however, it is always important to consider the likely impact of the message on audiences other than those it is directly intended for. A simple example of this was the furore created by an internal instruction within the advertising agency Ogilvy & Mather to amend a transparency of Ford workers for the Polish market. Whereas in the UK the photograph had shown an ethnically diverse mix of people, in Poland it was felt appropriate to retouch the transparency to make the workers look Caucasian and thereby reflect the local workforce. However, Ford and Ogilvy overlooked the impact of such a change on the UK workforce, who found out about the change. Ford's race relations policy was called into question and the company was severely criticised on television and in the press. A 'what if . . .' question might just have averted the whole fiasco.

The importance of feedback loops

One of the key aspects of the corporate branding model is the recognition of inter-relatedness. Although there is a flow from the identity through communications to the image, there are also ebbs. The marketing communications strategy, although based on the reality of the identity, is a dynamic force. The strategy will often be trying to shift awareness or perceptions of the company. In so doing it helps to change the way managers see the company itself. Similarly the employees' view of the identity will be determined by the cultural milieu, but the culture will change in response to the beliefs and actions of individuals. Some companies encourage a culture which is welcoming of the process of change, but it is still important that core values are maintained. One of the valuable roles of the internal communications process is thus the retention and reinforcement of the corporate culture. Further along in the integrated approach, marketing communications receive backward flows from various audiences. Suppliers and buyers will interact on a one-to-one basis and will let their views of the organisation and its communications be known. Companies regularly research the views of other audiences, such as consumers and institutional investors, to establish the efficacy of their marketing. The feedback they receive will lead to regular reviews of communications, and their amendment if necessary. Employees, especially if they are customer facing, will also be recipients of feedback. For example, someone who works in a shop quickly gets to know the attitudes of consumers towards the retailer. This in turn can lead to behaviour modification which can either be positive or negative. The requirement for management is to recognise that the feedback loops are there – whether they be formal or informal – and to use them to improve their understanding of the perspectives of the organisation's stakeholders. That understanding can lead to the building of relationships which can enhance corporate performance. As the American management guru, Henry Mintzberg, has shown, strategy is not a static process, rather it is emergent and subject to adaptation. Rather than a 'top down' definition of planning and management, organisational feedback tends to amend strategies as they evolve.[8]

The analytical process – uncovering the identity

The organisational identity is not something that can be uncovered by simple quantitative research techniques – although these can be an aid to

QUEEN MARGARET UNIVERSITY
COLLEGE LIBRARY

decision making. The emphasis is very much on a qualitative approach that allows us to understand the deeper values of the organisation. As noted earlier, the basic assumptions that determine corporate culture tend to become unconscious – rooting them out and understanding their cause is not an easy process. The sort of issues one is trying to resolve in this phase of research are the attributes that determine behaviour. In an attempt to deconstruct the organisation, the behavioural characteristics have to be defined. For example, an organisation might seem to encourage a high degree of confrontation, which can be observed through group discussions or attendance at meetings. The question to resolve, then, is to establish why confrontation is tolerated. The possibilities are a weak leader who fails to impose authority on warring factions or a belief that confrontation is good for generating excitement and enthusiasm or a powerful commitment to the principle that good ideas are worth fighting for. Once research has determined the rationale for confrontation, then the source of that belief needs to be determined. In the case of 'good ideas are worth fighting for', it may be because at some time in the organisation's evolution a good idea was ignored and an opportunity lost. As one digs down from observable behaviour, the values and assumptions of the organisation become apparent. As an example of this analytical process, Dr John Balmer undertook a major piece of research into the identity of BBC Scotland. His main research technique was action research, which works on the assumption that the best way to learn about an organisation is to participate in its evolution. Balmer found when he probed into the identities of two of the BBC's radio stations that the social psychological process of corporate identity formation was multilayered and extremely complex. This suggested that to view the BBC's identity as universal would be mistaken. The organisation, looking in from the viewpoint of subsidiaries, demonstrated a variety of cultures with different views and allegiances. Balmer found seven sub-cultures within the radio stations, which he defines as affinities:

> The data revealed that both stations were underpinned by distinct ideologies to which personnel had an affinity . . . . The data showed that personnel had an affinity to an ideology for various reasons. For instance an affinity based on closeness, nostalgia, affection, etc. Furthermore personnel had an affinity to non-corporate as well as corporate ideologies.[9]

Balmer comes to the conclusion that managers need to be sensitive to the various ideologies in an organisation and to nurture those which underpin the core values (Figure 4.3).

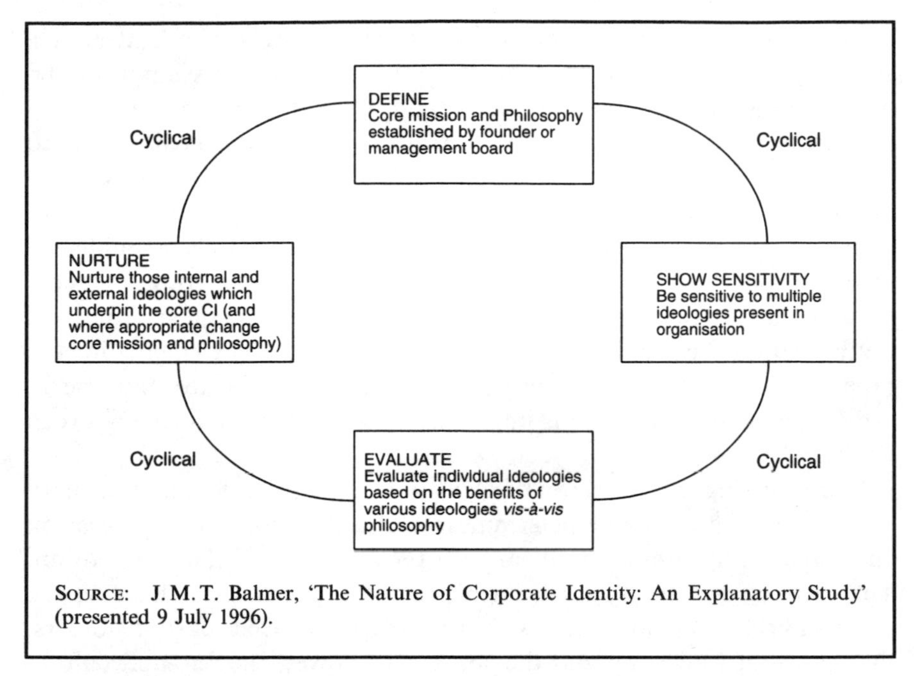

SOURCE: J. M. T. Balmer, 'The Nature of Corporate Identity: An Explanatory Study' (presented 9 July 1996).

Figure 4.3 Synthesis of the basic social processes involved in the adoption of a strategic corporate identity (CI)

However, before stepping inside an organisation, the first and most obvious step in the research process is to undertake desk research. This process involves the collation and assessment of all forms of written communication:

- documents and manuals
- statements of policy
- official histories
- marketing communications materials
- personnel policies – including reward systems
- previously undertaken primary research
- annual reports and accounts
- published performance data.

This process will provide indicators of the corporate values and how they are communicated. However, this does not negate the importance of following up the desk research, as the stated principles of the organisation may be far from the truth and closer to myths than reality. It is not uncommon, for organisations to build myths about themselves. In the early period of cultural formation, the seeming insight of a leader, or a successful way of working, becomes adopted as a core assumption. To help sustain that assumption, the organisational hierarchy constantly reinforces the myth that created it in the first place. If the media comes to believe in the myth, then it comes to be seen as an unassailable truth – a bond that can be very uncomfortable for the organisation to have to confront. The researcher who relies only on desk research or published media comment will only uncover the myth, not the truth, nor the motivations for the original assumption. This is not to suggest that the myth should be discarded, if it is an important element in the organisation's success – the recommendation might be to reinforce it, rather than expose it, but it is important to know the difference between truth and fiction.

Remembering the definition of identity this phase of desk and primary research is concerned with determining the 'facts' about the organisation and importantly comparing them with the attributes of the competition. The facts we are trying to unearth are the organisational history, the quality of the technology and its ability to meet the needs of stakeholders, the nature of leadership and the sources of power, the parental culture and relevant sub-cultures, the organisational strategy and its credibility given the available resources and skills, performance in terms of growth, profitability and turnover, the structures and systems and their orientation and finally the nature of the reward system. All of these need to be seen in the context of an ever-changing environment, the future direction of the organisation and the relevance of the attributes to stakeholders. It is little use having an identity that is built around highly engineered and expensive products if these matter little to customers. The difficulty for the organisation and any consultants, is separating out the reality from perceptions. For example, management may perceive that their technology is better than the competition, but objective measures, such as benchmarking, may show otherwise. The Japanese belief in benchmarking as a guide to establishing performance and judging progress is well known, and it is becoming more common in Europe. A pan-European research study revealed that benchmarking is one of the key requirements of successful companies. In reporting the results, Professor Amin Rajan stated:

> A pan-European study carried out jointly by the European Foundation for Management Development and my own organisation CREATE, showed that, irrespective of size, industrial background, legal status or ownership structure, nine out of ten UK companies are keen to engage

Table 4.2 Benchmarking

Automobile assembly plant productivity (units = hours/vehicle)	*Best*	*Average*
Japanese in Japan	13.2	16.8
Japanese in N. America	18.8	20.9
United States in N. America	18.6	24.9
United States and Japan in Europe	22.8	35.3
Europeans in Europe	22.8	35.5
Newly Industrializing Countries	25.7	41.0

SOURCE: J. P. Womack, D. T. Jones and D. Roos, *The Machine That Changed the World: The Story of Lean Production* (Harper Perennial, 1991) p. 85.

> in benchmarking. These results were broadly similar across all European Union member states.
>
> One in five successful companies are now doing some form of benchmarking, whereas five years ago they were doing hardly any. These companies are not insular, they are eager to learn from those who are the best in their class.[10]

The obvious point about the benchmarking process is that it provides a focus for change. It enables companies to judge their performance against the competition and to set standards. For example the drive to improve productivity in automotive manufacturing is the recognition of the success of the Japanese in this respect. For the last decade, European and American manufacturers have sought to emulate the practices of Toyota, Nissan and Honda – and they have improved as a result, even if Japan still leads the way. The reasons for this are complex, but essentially the principles of lean production, although effective in any culture, seem to have the best match in Japan (see Table 4.2).

The final point to note about the research methodology here is that although some elements of the research do not need to be carried out on a regular basis, others do. Performance measures need to be kept on an on-going basis and constantly compared with the best in the market.

Evaluating the corporate brand image

As noted already, organisations communicate all the time. To determine the impact of communications on audiences we need relevant research methods. The most obvious of these is the evaluation of the awareness of the corporate brand, both prompted and unprompted. The useful aspects of this research are when one company's performance is compared to the competition and the trend data over time. The difficulty in using this research in isolation is that it is often difficult to determine the source of awareness. A company could achieve high awareness ratings because it manufactures frequently purchased products, because its products are very visible, because it is good at generating press comment, because it spends a lot on advertising or because it has a strong message presented consistently. Sometimes it is possible to single out the specific impact of advertising or PR or product design and each service industry has its own communication effectiveness awards, built around the premise that the impact is identifiable, but the real test of the efficacy of a corporate image is in the measures, further up MORI's scale: trust, transaction, satisfaction, loyalty, advocacy (see Table 4.1, p. 49). These measures can be obtained through quantitative research, but the depth that can be achieved through qualitative studies is invaluable in understanding the nature and depth of relationship between a corporate brand and its audiences.

Consumers

With some organisations, where the link between the corporate brand and its products is low key, such as Unilever or Grand Metroplitan, the perceptions of the parent may be poor. Indeed Grand Metropolitan is still perceived by many to be a hotel chain – perhaps partly because its name suggests it – in spite of its withdrawal from the hotel business in the 1980s. Similarly people may have an awareness that Unilever is in the business of producing soaps and detergents, but the awareness may not go much deeper. In organisations where the corporate brand and its products or services are more overtly linked, the awareness of the organisation is likely to be stronger, but largely determined by the experience of product usage.

To uncover consumers' deeper feelings about a corporate brand, a combination of group discussions and one-to-one interviews can be used. Here we are not primarily concerned about consumer awareness, but the consumer relationship:

- what is the depth of feeling about the company
- what is the source of that feeling
- what is its personality
- how is this formed

- what is the relative importance of people, product and communications
- is the company to be trusted
- would consumers recommend the company to others?

None of these attributes tends to be front of mind and researchers sometimes employ association techniques to help draw out people's beliefs. These tend to take the form of relating the organisation to colours, images, animals or cars.

The financial community

How the financial community (individual and institutional investors, market analysts, bankers and brokers) sees a company is driven by perceptions of its management, its historical performance, its reputation, the industry it operates in and the relevance of its strategy. Financial perceptions are based on a judgement of profitability and turnover and more qualitative assessments of the company's potential. Work by Richard Higgins and Brendan Bannister (1992)[11] shows that market analysts place great importance on how effectively a company communicates its corporate strategy to them. Anecdotal evidence from *Fortune* magazine shows that there is a link between reputation and return to investors. This is borne out by international research by Opinion Research Corporation (ORC) among 4000 businesses in 18 countries which demonstrates the importance of an organisation's reputation and the management of that reputation. The executives interviewed agreed fairly universally with the following statements:

- when several companies' products or services are similar in quality or price, the companies' respective corporate reputations often determine which service the customer will buy
- a strong corporate reputation can sustain a company in times of controversy
- a company's reputation has financial value that is generally not appreciated
- a company's reputation needs to be managed as carefully as any other asset

and disagreed with,

- there isn't much a company can do to improve its image beyond that of its industry in general.

The interesting aspect of the research is its international consistency and for the conclusions reached about the impact of reputation on stock prices:

> Analysis of companies with higher corporate equity scores (based on six drivers of corporate reputation) reveals a strong correlation between more positive corporate reputations and higher price/earnings ratios in the financial marketplace. More specifically the ORC findings show the average corporate equity score for companies in the top third of P/E ratios is 62, in the second third 51, and in the bottom third 34.
>
> Moreover, a separate financial analysis by ORC of changes in stock price over a several year period indicates that some 8%–15% of a company's stock price (among selective companies analyzed) can be accounted for by corporate reputation.[12]

Researching financial audiences uses both qualitative and quantitative measures. Some companies conduct regular surveys of the attitudes of brokers and analysts. This can shed light on overall perceptions towards the organisation and highlight any areas for concern. Again it is both the performance of competitors and the trends over time that is really useful. One-off research will provide data, but without points of comparison, there will be no way of telling whether the results are good or bad. In addition to the survey process, companies also conduct one-to-one interviews with relevant audiences. Focus groups are inappropriate here, partly because of the practical problem of getting people together, but also because of the nature of the subject and the people interviewed. In-depth research attempts to uncover what analysts feel about a company's prospects, about the quality of its communications and importantly its image. Some of the more cynical executives doubt the validity of this process, because they believe that too many analysts' judgements are based on superficial analyses and herd-like instincts, but this ignores the importance of the corporate brand image. Even if analysts do fulfil people's worse fears, their views are a key determinant of share values. In the USA the importance of explaining the corporate brand seems to be rated more highly than in Europe. Partly this is because whatever the short-termist ills of quarterly reporting, the frequency of having to communicate performance keeps management's relationships with their investors and brokers at the front of their minds. Secondly, in terms of stakeholder importance, shareholders seem to have greater prominence in the USA.

Suppliers and buyers

The power of the corporate brand relative to its suppliers and buyers determines the nature of relationships. This at least is the traditional view. Michael Porter in developing his five-forces model of industry attractiveness, suggested that two of the key drivers were the power of buyers and the power of suppliers. This seems logical. If a company is a dominant force in its industry, whereas its suppliers and buyers are fragmented, it will be able to dictate the terms of business. And once the suppliers or buyers become dependent, then the company can begin to impose more stringent arrangements. In the UK, this situation is typical of retailer–supplier relationships. The concentration of retail power in relatively few hands has allowed the major multiples to squeeze their suppliers and in such areas as groceries this has led to high margins relative to European supermarkets. The implication for the corporate brand is to concentrate its buying resources. Rather than having multiple buying centres or buying based in divisions, it makes more sense to have a unified buying source (and identity) that can wield more power over its suppliers. When Courtaulds underwent an identity programme in the late 1980s, which resulted in a single brand name for all its businesses, part of the benefit was in the impact on buyers. The then identity manager said: 'it [the corporate identity programme] has certainly enabled us to explain the spread of our businesses more easily than we could before, both to the City and to our big customers.' As Porter notes, this is because of the potential for inter-relationships:

> A firm should develop both its corporate identity as well as those of its business units, within the firm and outside. This not only affects management's view of themselves, but can directly facilitate the achievement of market inter-relationships by making buyers more aware of the connection between business units.[13]

While it is important to communicate the strength of the corporate brand to suppliers and buyers, in recent years more and more emphasis has been placed on the idea of alliances (an area of significant and rapid growth) and on partnership sourcing. This is a significant departure from Porter's ethos, the whole tenor of which is adversarial and competitive. Some are now arguing for the idea of a composite strategy:

> An all or nothing choice between a single-minded striving for either competitive or collaborative advantage would, however, be a false one.

> Neither a totally adversarial stance on all fronts or an entirely collaborative approach is necessarily – or likely to be – an optimal course of action for any firm. The real strategic choice problem that all businesses face is where (and how much) to collaborate, and where (and how intensely) to act competitively.[14]

The idea of partnership sourcing is not a new one. The Japanese keiretsu system is founded on the idea of relationships between nominally separate organisations, who come together to organise distribution, share capital and use technology. One of the complaints of European and US companies is that this 'insider system' hinders foreign companies from selling their products. Although this closed web possibly hinders consumer choice, the huge benefit to Japanese companies is that it allows them to focus on their core strengths. Toyota is one of the largest car manufacturers in the world, yet it has less than a tenth of the workers of General Motors. Partly this is to do with productivity, but it also a lot to do with sub-contracting out large parts of the production process to its supplier partners:

> Toyota is the lead company in a so-called vertical keiretsu, itself performing only design and final assembly functions. It is, however, linked with hundreds of independent subcontractors and parts suppliers in an informal but durable network.[15]

The keiretsu approach has been replicated in other parts of the world, partly through partnership based out-sourcing in such areas as information technology and clinical research and partly through closer working relationships between companies and their suppliers. The problem for Western companies has been the seeming risks involved in relying on partners outside the formal company network. As Fukuyama points out, the key advantage that the Japanese enjoy is the high levels of socially-defined trust that are simply not evident to the same degree in Western cultures, where companies have sometimes been resistant to the idea of placing trust in other organisations and relying on others to work to similar standards. However, research among 400 companies by the Confederation of British Industry (CBI) and the consulting firm Arthur D. Little (1995) found increasing evidence of partnerships at work:

- 97% of companies are aware of partnership sourcing
- 91% understand the concept
- 83% believe that partnership sourcing will have a significant impact on competitiveness

- 74% have implemented partnerships
- of those in partnerships 80% use them for purchasing.[16]

The researchers note that:

> power issues between buyer and seller are still a concern as comments from respondents indicate. Some buyers call their cooperation with the supplier 'partnership', whereas the supplier sees the relationship quite differently . . . Power issues are of concern where the supplier's products are easily substitutable and of low value to the customer.[17]

However the overwhelming conclusion of the report is that partnership sourcing has been successful in fostering competitiveness and that companies who have set up real partnerships are now benefiting in 'the key areas of cost, quality and time'.

What are the implications for the corporate brand? Companies need to reject the traditional adversarial relationship in favour of agreement on common goals and a commitment to learning from partners. This requires trust and a willingness to expend effort in improving communication. Indeed the CBI/Arthur D. Little study shows that the core features of partnerships are in such areas as regular process meetings, exchange of suggestions about product and process improvements and cross-functional teamwork. Visual identities are unlikely to be altered, unless the partnership results in a strategic alliance or merger, but internally there are likely to be requirements to change the culture away from a closed system to one where open book accounting and the sharing of ideas become the norm. The experience of Kodak with one of its key suppliers, Croda Celluloids, shows that cultural change is one of the key barriers to overcome: 'changing the culture internally, the crucial foundation for a successful partnership requires a considerable amount of time.'[18]

The need to collaborate does not undermine the validity of the Porter model, which remains a valuable guide to industry attractiveness, but it does suggest a limitation of the model as a guide to strategy. If companies are willing to enter into partnerships then the power relationship needs to be understood, but it should not dictate action. The more pressing requirement is the self-analysis to understand the cultural issues that may prevent a successful approach to partnerships and a thorough analysis of likely partners. The latter should comprise research into the hard facts about the partner, in terms of performance and quality and also some of the softer issues, such as human resource policy and image. The benefits of partnership can be significant, but there are inherent dangers if the partner under-performs and the image of the company is tarnished as a result.

Media, government and other influencers

Journalists, politicians, civil servants and administrators of influential bodies may be relatively small in number compared to a consumer audience, but their power is enormous even if, as MORI research shows, the public's trust in what they say is strictly limited: 10% trust journalists and 11% government ministers. The power of the media, for instance, is nowhere better illustrated than Jon Entine's exposé of The Body Shop in *Business Ethics* in September 1994.[19] His critique of the company's products and policies led to widespread coverage in the press, and tarnished The Body Shop's reputation as a socially responsible organisation. The power of journalists to destroy or raise the status of a company suggests that organisations should do everything in their power to nurture relationships with the media – to provide honest and truthful information on an on-going basis and to be as supportive as possible. Companies that are good at this either, because of individual high profiles, such as Richard Branson of Virgin, or because of corporate policy can reap the benefits of a clear and positive corporate image. Those who do not often claim they are unfairly represented or ignored.

Similarly good relations with politicians and civil servants is important in several respects. First, it helps organisations to be aware of government thinking which may impinge on the economic or legal environment. Second, it provides organisations with the opportunity to have their views heard and to become influential in policy making. Third, acquisitions – especially ones that have a political dimension – are more likely to have a smoother ride if the organisation has a positive image. The latter was always a problem for Lonrho after it had been dubbed 'the unacceptable face of capitalism' during the early 1970s.

Outside of government, in every country and within the European Community, there are bodies that represent various interest groups. As groups with memberships in their own right, they carry influence, but there is also value in their lobbying power and their ability to help transform opinion. When conducting research into the corporate brand all the above people have an important part to play in establishing a positive reputation, and consequently their views should be sought. The difficulty for the researcher is that these audiences are difficult to reach and tend to be over-researched. The only viable route is qualitative work in the form of one-to-one interviews.

Local communities

The final audience of the corporate brand are the local communities within which a company operates. Most often the company will be one of many employers, but in some cases a large company comes to dominate a community. In this instance, its relationship with local people will be vital to success. Companies that accrue a positive local reputation benefit from being seen as an integral part of a community and consequently can attract the best people to work for them. They might also enjoy high consumption of their products, have a good image in the local media and be seen to be contributing to the local environment. Research by MORI showed the following spontaneous responses to the question 'what kinds of social responsibilities, if any, do you think companies have?'

	(%)
• look after employees/good pay and conditions	40
• protect the local environment	21
• reduce/stop pollution	14
• good service to consumers	13
• fair prices	12
• provide good pensions/healthcare for employees	12
• be honest and reliable	10
• involvement in local community/sponsorship of local events	10

The interesting aspect of this research is that emphasis is given to employee pay and conditions, whereas local community involvement is rated lower. However, two things should be noted here. First, community involvement should be seen as vital to corporate well-being, because as Sir Iain Vallance, Chairman of BT, observes:

> our business depends considerably on the health of the community. If that is adversely affected by deprivation, crime, vandalism, racial tension, inner-city decay, homelessness or pollution, so too is our own business health.[20]

The second potential benefit is that companies who are good corporate citizens find that it has a significant impact on the morale of employees. Those people within the organisation who become actively involved also seem to perform more effectively. Research by Prima Europe came to the view that corporate community involvement 'yields business benefits, particularly in communication, team working and influencing skills'.

Research results

The conclusion to the qualitative and quantitative research into the attitudes and motivations of the organisation's various audiences will be an image of the organisation. Experience suggests that although there will be some common elements of image that stretch across all audiences, there will also be variances with each audience and indeed within each audience. So underlying the overall image there will be a set of specific images. Partly this is desirable; within an overall framework companies should be tailoring their messages to ensure their relevance to a specific audience. Partly it is inevitable; each individual and group has a different set of cultural assumptions and the interpretation of a message depends on what one believes in and one's self-interest. Partly it is mismanagement; generally, companies do not communicate as well as they think they do. Of course, it is impossible to control all the messages all the time, but there is often inconsistency in external communications – with, for example, a piece of literature tonally and literally contradicting what is being said in advertising. This is a result of fragmentation in the management of the organisation's communications. Also, if organisations fail to understand their own competence and culture they will produce communications which cannot be substantiated by performance, and in particular by the actions of employees. This thinking is at the heart of the suggested research methodology. For by comparing the organisational 'reality' – or the identity – with perceptions – or image – we can begin to see whether the corporate brand is being accurately represented: whether communications are supporting the organisational strategy, are culturally credible and relevant to all the brand's stakeholders. If the image and identity are misaligned, dissonance is created and corrective action, either in organisational performance or communications, or both, needs to be taken.

Summary

The model described in this chapter provides a structure for looking at the corporate brand. Its value is in ensuring that internal and external communications are tied together to help create an advantageous and sustainable positioning for the organisation. It recognises the diversity of audiences an organisation has to communicate with and the flux of the market environment. The model should be able to evolve as culture and circumstances change. Its interaction with external factors and the feedback loops should ensure that the identity and image are in constant adaptation, without changing the fundamental values that drive the organisation, except in an evolutionary way. Of course, whatever the validity of the model, organisations need to have the resources, structures, people and commitment to communication. Feedback loops are credible only if the organisation has the ability to listen to what it hears and the desire to act upon what it discovers.

5 Defining a Corporate Branding and Communications Strategy

The research process enables an organisation to determine a corporate branding strategy. This is more complex than a brands strategy because, as Chapter 4 has shown, organisations have a wide diversity of audiences who may have countervailing interests. The corporate branding strategy has to determine the relationships – both actual and visual – between the component parts of the organisation and with all audiences. It needs to recognise the people and the product issues of the corporate brand. It needs to work with the strengths and weaknesses of the corporate culture. And it needs to support the organisational strategy. This chapter will address two core issues: the nature of corporate branding structure and the ways and means of developing a corporate communications strategy. In the case of the former, the main requirement is to develop a structure that reflects the nature of the organisation and its priorities. This can either be corporate brand dominant or brands dominant. The corporate identity research programme, outlined in Chapter 4, will act as a guide to which structure is most appropriate.

Monolithic corporate brands

The main determinant of image for a service provider, such as Virgin, is in the quality of its employees. Achieving consistency of employee performance is hard to achieve, but is a fundamental element in attaining a cohesive corporate brand image. The other key element is the visual branding. Virgin is what has been called a 'monolithic brand'. Products, from cola to vodka to insurance to airlines are branded Virgin. This

Box 5.1 The long-sighted and the myopic enterprise

Plan and operate the enterprise so as to enable its key assets, its people, to work at their very best. This governs the priorities of the business, its size and style. We give top priorities to the interests of our staff; second priority to those of our customers; third to our shareholders. This is not only a reflection of the importance of our people, it is also the most positive way of fitting together these three priorities. Working backwards the interests of our shareholders depend upon high levels of customer satisfaction . . . which depends on high standards of service from our people, which depends on happy staff who are proud of the company they work for. We are all familiar with what happens when these priorities are reversed. A myopic enterprise, which gives top priority to the short term interests of its shareholders, sacrifices employees' job security, rewards and working environment. This starts a chain of negative consequences, eroding pride, goodwill and enthusiasm. Poor performance by demotivated and antagonised employees erodes service quality and customer satisfaction and in the end the long-term interests of shareholders are actually damaged by giving them superficial short-term priority.[1]

Richard Branson, Virgin

allows Virgin to use its powerful corporate image to confer credibility on its new ventures – often in markets where it has no previous reputation. This idea of a wide-ranging corporate brand is not uncommon in Japan, where companies such as Yamaha have long demonstrated the potential to stretch brands across widely differing product areas. However, it is relatively rare in Europe, where the trend is towards greater business focus, not diversity. What enables Virgin to achieve success in such different markets is the clarity of its corporate branding. Virgin is not transferring a particular competence from airlines to cola, but an image of youth, dynamism and quality. In this respect it is acting almost like a fashion brand. For the right target market Virgin offers a bundle of appealing values. Of course, if an individual is seeking stability and conservatism, Virgin is probably not for them.

The other core benefit monolithic branding confers is economies of communication. Every time one sees a Virgin advertisement or product it is reinforcing the corporate image, not only for consumers but also for financial, media and governmental audiences. If all of Virgin's products had different brand names, this simply wouldn't happen. The monolithic approach to the corporate brand is in many ways ideal, but is difficult to achieve and is not without dangers. One of Branson's core principles is to build businesses, not buy them. Organic growth makes it much easier to build one cohesive corporate brand than if one is acquiring companies. Often in an acquisition, an organisation is buying a brand name, thus it would seem foolhardy to immediately dispense with the name, post-purchase, simply to ensure that the brand fitted neatly into a branding scheme. Sometimes the decision to discard a well established brand name is taken in the longer-term interests of consistency and economies of communication, but unless the process is handled with sensitivity there is the possibility of damaging the brand's relationships with its audiences.

The danger of linking everything under one brand name is the greater potential for linkages to be made if there is an adverse event. It is always important to remember that branding is a two-way relationship. In determining whether to link a parent company closely with a brand, the value the parent name adds to the brand has to be considered, as does the value the brand adds to the parent. When the linkage is overt, bad and good news are more immediately connected. Companies may also find it more difficult to withdraw from a market if a business unit or division has the same name. Although further down the branding hierarchy, this is the problem that Unilever faced in transferring the name of their highly successful detergent brand, Persil onto their washing up liquid brand. In a market dominated by Procter & Gamble's Fairy Liquid, Unilever felt their only opportunity to dent Fairy's market share was to use a well established brand name. They prevaricated for the best part of a decade before deciding to put Persil onto washing up liquid, because they recognised that once they did so, withdrawal from the market was not an option lest the failure in this sector impacted on the image of the Persil detergent brand. Although monolithic brands enjoy many advantages, not least the ease with which they can explain the spread of their businesses to specific audiences such as shareholders and suppliers, more diversified brands can still enjoy many of the same advantages, if they work hard to explain the spread of their businesses. However it is difficult to imagine Virgin succeeding to the same degree if it had adopted a diversified branding approach: why should anyone buy a cola or vodka, in preference to established brands, without the added value of the Virgin name?

The branded approach

The alternative to the Virgin approach is that adopted by Tube Investments. Tube Investments (TI) was formed in 1919 and was for many years Britain's second largest engineering company. During its growth the company acquired a series of famous brand names, such as Raleigh (bicycles) and Russell Hobbs, Creda and Glow Worm (appliances). The acquisition-based approach and the strength of the individual brand names encouraged TI to promote the brand names rather than that of the parent. Most of these brands have in fact been sold in the last 10 years, as TI has left behind its consumer goods past for a more engineering-based organisation with two core corporate brands: Bundy and John Crane. These two businesses account for almost all of TI's £2.5 billion value. Historically, TI endorsed its businesses, so that it was clear to people that Raleigh, for example, was part of TI – a fact that mattered little to consumer audiences but may have had some residual impact on shareholders, employees and suppliers, but the essence of the TI structure has been brand dominant. There is clearly a rationale for the structure, but the more interesting debate is its relative strengths and weaknesses. A branded approach is widely used in fast-moving consumer goods marketing, because it allows companies, such as Unilever and Procter & Gamble to segment markets and deliver targeted products unencumbered by parental branding. It is used by conglomerates, who want to buy and sell companies and therefore retain the power and independence of a corporate brand. It is used by companies that have grown through acquisition, and have been reticent to discard the power of individual brands.

Although there have been some examples of de-mergers, which has led to a fragmentation of a single corporate brand (such as ICI and Zeneca) the norm is for companies to move towards more unified structures. Generally they are more cohesive and easier to explain – especially to professional audiences. If TI could handle the transition to a monolithic approach without damaging its core businesses, then it would probably gain some communication benefits. This is not to de-value the branded route when it is appropriate, but for most companies there is greater merit in being monolithic.

Nonetheless a more branded structure does provide other benefits. Smaller and more accessible business units can allow the development of a closer relationship between employees as well as consumers and the brand. According to MORI about three-quarters of people believe that 'as they grow bigger, companies usually get cold and impersonal in their relations with people'. Certainly within a company such as Grand Metropolitan, with its branded structure, there is considerable loyalty to business units, such as the drinks division, IDV. If the process is properly managed it is possible to achieve clear identification with a smaller business unit, while still communicating corporate brand strength to audiences that need to know. Pepsico, for example, has a number of well known brands as well as Pepsi-Cola, such as Pizza Hut and Taco Bell. There is an obvious link between the main brand and its parent, but the other products are not clearly linked, except when the company wants to convey its size, such as when it is communicating to governmental audiences. Then all the company brand names are featured under the Pepsico banner.

Another scenario which is appropriate to a branded structure is when a company's reputation in one field overshadows or is irrelevant to its brands. Then it makes sense to separate the corporate ownership from that of the brand – it will either confuse the communication or communicate a negative image. One further cited benefit of the branded structure is that bad news is less obviously linked when a parent and its brand operate under separate names. There may be an element of truth in this, but the pervasiveness of media comment tends to ensure that connections are made. Certainly when Cunard was severely criticised for sailing its flagship, the QE2 in a state of semi-repair, there was also condemnation of its parent, Trafalgar House.

Endorsed corporate brands

The in-between status in corporate structures is the endorsed route. This allows companies to mix and match their approach to branding. Some parts of the organisation can be overtly linked while others are kept separate or alternately the linkage is less obvious because the brand or business unit is the dominant element, while there is some form of subsidiary corporate branding in the form of a graphic or description, such as 'company *x* is a member of the *y* group'. The use of endorsements is a valid approach provided it is in response to corporate objectives, rather than something that has been allowed to develop without real consideration of the benefits of the most effective branding structure. In reality the latter is probably the most common situation. Until the security and banknote printer, De La Rue, underwent a corporate branding review it possessed some 240 different companies under a wide diversity of brand names – some of which were prefixed by 'De La Rue', but some of which had no obvious connection. It was a situation that had arisen from an acquisitive era in the company's history which had stressed the importance of operational autonomy rather than cohesion.

Defining the most appropriate structure

How, then, to decide the most appropriate brand structure for an organisation? The following suggest a more monolithic structure:

- an emphasis on organic growth
- a need to emphasise the points of commonality within an organisation
- the need to communicate globally
- a tightly defined identity built around closely related businesses or a clearly defined idea
- the potential for economies of communication
- the parent brand has a strong reputation.

A more branded structure is best when:

- the emphasis is on acquisitive growth
- the organisation's strength is in its brands
- there is a need to segment audiences
- there is a wide diversity of businesses within the corporate portfolio.

Whichever structure is chosen or is dictated by circumstance, there is still the potential to obviate the weaknesses of the structure. For example, even if an organisation has a branded structure which makes it harder to communicate its strength to financial audiences by natural linkage, it should do everything in its power to compensate for this by corporate advertising, presentations and PR. Or, similarly, if industry globalisation is encouraging companies to become more monolithic, yet an organisation has several strong brands, it can opt for an approach that puts the parent and brands together for a transition period.

The way an organisational structure is presented is not simply a result of determining priorities and then focusing the organisation to meet them. The structure is determined by (and also influences) history, strategy and the organisation's source of competitive advantage. Could one imagine Virgin as a branded company structure? Yes, but it would make rational sense only if it was venturing into markets, such as retirement homes, where its youthful reputation was of little relevance. And of course, it shouldn't be venturing into retirement homes, given the strength and focus of its reputation.

The communications strategy

Having looked at the nature of the organisation's structure, this needs to be incorporated into our thinking about its communications strategy. Communications strategy is about integration: the development of a coherent plan that is based upon the reality of the corporate identity and that creates a relevant image that can help an organisation meet its broader objectives. If the organisation has a monolithic structure, the requirement to be consistent in communications will be greater. Certainly, Virgin demonstrates strong points of consistency in the style and tone of its communications. In branded structures the communications are more likely to be diverse across the organisation, as each business unit focuses its attention on delivering relevant communications for itself, rather than the corporate whole.

Whether the organisation is monolithic or branded or somewhere in between, it needs to understand its true nature – what its culture enables it to achieve and what is strategically desirable. If either or both of these is out of kilter the organisation will develop a communication strategy that is unsustainable (the culture will contradict the message) or irrelevant. Similarly if the desired image is inappropriate an organisation will not position itself in an optimal way. Apart from one or two exceptions, the insurance industry is full of communication campaigns which present rosy images which are blatantly contradicted by experience of insurance companies. This is communication strategy based on wishful thinking rather than reality. Cynicism rather than trust is the result.

Integration is also a rarely attained ideal. The premise here is that an organisation's audiences will not distinguish between the source of a message. It matters little to a consumer as to whether the message they receive is through a piece of literature or advertising or media comment (although this may have seemingly more credibility because of its independence). The collective whole will form a picture in the mind of the beholder. This is not to suggest that messages are always slavishly the same, but that the style and tone should always be consistent. This holistic view is why some organisations do try to integrate communications and why advertising agencies form integrated divisions. However, it is only the enlightened few who also integrate the behavioural aspects of communications – what employees say and do – into the whole. The reasons for this are two-fold. First, in most companies the human resource function is distinct from the marketing function. Second the agencies who advise on integrated campaigns deal primarily in paid-for media – their focus and expertise is not on organisational development or training. To overcome these barriers companies need to ensure that the 'people aspect' of their communications is fully integrated with marketing communications. This is supported by research undertaken by New York-based consultancy Lippincott & Margulies:

> The firm's research on how employees impact a desired change consistently shows that employees' feelings can significantly affect the opinions of external audiences toward the company along with its products and services.[2]

The characteristics of communications strategy

Communication strategies should always be a unique reflection of an organisation, but there are points of continuity, which should be evident in all strategies.

Strategies should be consistent and long lasting

One of the key temptations in strategy formulation is the desire to keep searching for a competitive advantage. It is of course true that both organisations and the environment in which they operate are constantly changing and that this sometimes invalidates a communication strategy, but successful corporate brands such as Virgin and Nike seem to sustain long-lasting positions in spite of this. All too often an organisation will find it is losing market share, and as a result will review its strategy. Research will then be used to define a new approach. Both the organisation and its advisors will tend to have a vested interest in change and the research will be concerned with determining a new strategy. Alternatives will be evaluated to decide which is likely to be the most effective. Rarely will new strategies be evaluated in comparison with the existing one, which in everyone's mind will already have been discarded. Once the process starts it gathers a momentum of its own which precludes a return to the previous strategy. Burger King, in its attempt to find a competitive position against McDonald's, went through 17 different advertising campaigns and 5 agencies between 1975 and 1994 without finding the basis for an on-going strategy. Similarly, Smirnoff had 10 different campaigns in the USA in the 16 years to 1995 and a market share decline of 5 percentage points.[3] In the same period, Absolut had one campaign based around the image of a bottle and two words, one of which was 'Absolut'. In 10 years the brand went from selling 12 000 cases a year to US brand leader in the imported vodka sector with sales of 2.7 million cases. The marketing world is littered with Burger Kings and Smirnoffs.

Consistency in communication is a virtuous circle. Most often it is achieved because an organisation has a clear and focused idea of what it stands for and how it wants to be seen. The consistency then reinforces the brand values to both external and internal audiences. When a company has achieved a virtuous circle, it tends not to go out searching for the elusive ideal campaign, it simply evolves what it has always done. The communications strategy can become almost intuitive – people know what feels right. Compare, for example, the schizophrenia of British Leyland/Austin/Rover Group advertising over recent decades with that of its acquirer, BMW. Over the last 30 years what has become known as Rover, has gone through a variety of transformations. The company has had different names, different brands and different communication strategies. Underlying this lack of consistency has been any clear understanding about the product itself and its positioning in the marketplace. It has gone from being a volume car maker to a specialist, from modern design to nostalgia and from a branded structure to a monolithic one. Apart from the distinctive and clearly branded Land Rover, the group has under-performed over a long period of time. BMW has also had difficult times. Pre-war it was known for the excellence of its engineering and performance, but by the late 1950s its product portfolio comprised ponderous and slow saloons and a bubble car made under licence from a Italian refrigerator manufacturer. Near to bankruptcy, the company was saved by two financiers, the Quandt brothers. Their money helped the company relaunch itself with a new model in 1962 that was the forerunner of the current 3 series. The key to the brand's renaissance was the commitment to the old principles of the company: performance and engineering. Even so, the development of BMW outside of its German market was still relatively slow. In the USA, by 1974, BMW was selling some 15 000 units, compared to Mercedes' 40 000. What transformed BMW from a cult brand to a more mainstream product was a campaign that was derived from BMW's philosophy and heritage and was executed in a consistent tone throughout the world for the next 20+ years. 'The Ultimate Driving Machine' campaign created by US agency Ammirati and Puris, was designed to communicate the idea that BMW was a luxury car that provided an exhilarating driving experience. The agency described the campaign as follows:

> We used performance as the foundation to change the standards by which everyone was judging luxury cars and as the basis for an entirely new automotive category. Until that point there had never been a 'luxury sports sedan'. Luxury cars either did their best to mimic the living room and isolate you from the driving experience or they were two seater sports cars.[4]

The strength of the approach was that whatever the message, the communications were guided by a consistent strategy. When there was increased consumer concern about safety in the 1980s, BMW changed the style of their advertising to address this concern. Whereas Volvo – true to their heritage – tackled the issue by stressing the robust construction of their cars, BMW chose to use its performance engineering background to communicate the idea of active safety: the range of wind tests and technical innovations, such as anti-lock brakes and new suspension systems, that could be used to avoid accidents.

Strategies should be distinctive

Having a distinctive communication strategy should not be an exercise in gratuitousness – distinctiveness must be based on organisational reality and relevance to stakeholders. When differentiation lacks substance then consumers and other audiences can ignore it. Take, for example, the desire of Pepsi-Cola to break away from cola own brands and Coca-Cola. In a market in which all major companies use red as a defining colour, Pepsi decided to relaunch with blue cans as a point of difference. With no change in the actual content or quality of the product, consumers seemed to have ignored the colour change, viewing it as a cosmetic device. In contrast, Hutchison Telecom's mobile telecommunications brand, Orange, is not only distinctively different in the simplicity of its presentation, the product is also perceived by many consumers as superior to the competition.

Points of difference need not be radical. In many markets, such as financial services, products may be remarkably similar, but subtle differences in service quality and presentation can be used to interest consumers and other audiences. Creating a perceptual difference can also be attributed to simply communicating attributes that the competition have failed to recognise are important. The Body Shop owns the area of environmentally friendly cosmetics because they have consistently marketed the company using this platform, whereas their rivals have been more diffident. In sports shoes the long-term rivals, Nike and

Reebok and the now resurgent Adidas have competed consistently on the basis of product quality and innovation. However the real point of differentiation comes from the subtly distinct ways in which the relative brands are positioned. As noted previously Nike has a streetwise, 'in your face' positioning which allows it to use controversial endorsees and confrontational advertising which is encapsulated by the 'Just do it' end line. In contrast, Reebok, which has traditionally been stronger with female buyers, has a softer caring image. Its endorsees are generally less controversial: soccer player Dennis Bergkamp, tennis player Arantxa Sanchez and ice skater, Nancy Kerrigan. Adidas, the one-time market leader, has been bouncing back under new management. Using its heritage, dating back to the 1920s, Adidas has begun to use the slogan 'We knew then. We know now'. When retro styling in sports shoes became fashionable, Adidas was perfectly positioned to reissue its classic ranges, while Nike had to try to invent heritage – something the Japanese have been trying to do with car design for a long time. The tone of the various advertising campaigns reflects the various organisational cultures, their areas of strength and the needs of the target markets. Distinctiveness has been achieved by the three brands, whereas the temptation must be to simply follow the approach of market leader, Nike.

Strategies should be single-minded and all-encompassing

The importance of integrating communications has been a consistent theme of this book. In communication strategy terms this does not suggest that all audiences should be treated in the same way. In fact, the suggestion is almost the opposite. Using the opportunity to segment audiences into clearly defined groups suggests tailored communications and relationship building rather than uniformity. The conundrum is, as Schumacher notes that 'we always need freedom and order'.[5] Thus the strategic requirement is to develop an overall message and tone to communications that clearly positions the organisation in the mind of all its audiences (always accepting that personal prejudice will define how the communication is 'read'). Within the order of the overall strategy there needs to be the freedom to tailor the message in such a way that it maximises the relevance to a reader, while still maintaining a sense of continuity. This is where communication programmes can become a straitjacket. In the desire for order – a not uncommon occurrence in large organisations where control can be difficult to achieve – communications can be too strictly defined, or in the parlance of identity programmes, policed. This is the experience of BT, whose late 1980s' identity review led to a system that rightly instilled discipline into the organisation. As BT has developed and become less rule-bound and more entreprenuerial there is now the desire to loosen the systems that control communications.

The process of defining a communications strategy

Communication strategies should always start from the need to meet specific and ideally quantifiable communication objectives. The overarching goal should be to achieve a specific positioning that will transcend the objectives for different audiences. The positioning itself should be derived from analysis. And it will need to encompass where the company sells its products or services, its attitudes to pricing and the design and performance of everything it produces. Of course, the approach will depend on the nature of the corporate branding structure. In the case of an fmcg company, where there is little link between the individual brands and the parent, the key requirement from a corporate perspective will be to order the relationships between the various brands. The corporate brand itself may be largely invisible to everyone except financial audiences, where the strength of the brand portfolio will be an important attribute. In instances where there are clear links between the brand(s) experienced by consumers and the parent, then the interrelationship will be an important determinant of the corporate image. In the case of the latter structure, the positioning of the individual brands and that of the parent need to be congruent. A successful retailer, such as the American department store group, Nordstrom, which has a strong reputation for its service and quality, would be unlikely to benefit from positioning a subsidiary under the same brand name as a low quality discounter.

The example of Cardin

It is possible to undermine a positioning by stretching a brand name too far. An example of this is the French fashion brand, Pierre Cardin. Cardin, who trained at Dior, opened his own fashion house in 1953. He was the first couturier to exploit the mass-market potential of his name and used his distinctive PC logotype on everything from bed linen to lingerie to perfumes and stockings. In the mid-1960s, Cardin was forced to resign from the Chambre Syndicale – the governing body of French couture – because he was undermining the exclusivity of French fashion. The idea of licensing has since been adopted by all major fashion brands, but the failing of Cardin as a brand was its lack of control. The over-exposure of the name and the type of retail outlets that sell the products reduced the quality image of the brand and its reputation as a couture house. Whereas more tightly controlled fashion brands have been more selective in distribution and maintained a premium for their brand name the Cardin name largely lost its cachet – and its premium. Now, to extend their brands, fashion companies tend to develop subsidiary brands, such as Donna Karan's DKNY, which has an obvious link to the main brand but offers its own range through specialist outlets. How then should the positioning be determined? In each market segment and for each audience there are attributes that matter. For executive saloon car buyers, comfort, status and quality are important. For utility shareholders, risk, liabilities, past performance and future strategies will be key influencers. In each case the nature of the options available defines the segment. By and large Rolls-Royce does not compete against Porsche in the mind of buyers – the attributes are different – but it may well compete against top-end Mercedes cars. Knowing what matters to buyers is determined by research and experience. The difficulty an organisation may face is that it finds itself poorly positioned relative to what people need and want. The debate then is how an organisation can change its position. Certainly, it should not indulge in wish-driven strategy: it has to understand the nature of its competency. Rolls-Royce might find that there is a growing demand for smaller engined executive cars, but if its competency is in highly engineered large engines, this may not be a viable need for it to answer. Alternatively, if the growing demand is for large engined but more modern looking cars, Rolls might define a strategy that moves its positioning gradually away from its more traditional look towards modernity. The inherent danger is that the company may lose some of its strength in so doing. It has also to recognise that the process of change may well take a long time to achieve, especially in the minds of buyers. Credible and effective positionings are determined by the correct match of market opportunity to competency – something that is easily stated, but hard to achieve in practice, especially given the volatility of markets. Another car manufacturer, Morgan, which has handbuilt essentially the same car since 1936, might at any stage in its long history have decided that it needed to modernise the look of its vehicles. Had it done so, it would have lost its appeal. Once a positioning has been defined, the organisation needs to gear itself up to communicate it consistently to all relevant audiences. If an organisation wants to be seen as modern and customer-oriented then its outlets, service, pricing, product and communications need to work together. The nature of the message may vary depending on the audience, but the essential positioning should not.

Communication mechanisms

The communication mechanisms open to organisations are changing. Whereas a decade ago the emphasis was very much on an advertising-led approach to communications, the revolution in information technology (IT) has meant that more direct forms of communication are growing. The key benefit of advertising was, and is, its ability to build awareness. As a medium it is good at communicating simple messages quickly and effectively. However, even with greater media specialisation which enables companies to communicate with more tightly defined audiences, advertising cannot deliver the same precision as direct marketing. Nor does it generate specific information on customers: it is a one way form of communication. This does not suggest that advertising has no long-term role to play. Advertising agencies, with their well developed structures, are most often the lead agencies in communication programmes and advertising has a key role to play in facilitating the effectiveness of other media. The often quoted press ad produced by the publisher McGraw-Hill to promote advertising in its corporate publications is good testament to the importance of awareness. In it, a gruff-looking man stares out from the page. The text cites a long list of reasons why he won't do business with a salesman – most of which revolve around the fact he doesn't know about the salesman's company. The long list of objections is finished off by the statement – 'now what was it you wanted to sell me'. Advertising cannot build trust in itself, but it can raise awareness and familiarity, which can lead to trust. If consumers have an awareness of the organisation, the propensity to look favourably on the company and its products is enhanced. MORI found when it asked people to agree/disagree with the statement, 'a company that has a good reputation would not sell poor products', that 60% agreed, 27% disagreed and 13% felt neither was appropriate. Similarly 31% of people say that they never buy products they have never heard of. Thus the maintenance of overall awareness of and the communication of the core positioning attributes is the key role of advertising.

Public relations (PR) activity fulfils a not dissimilar role to advertising, in that its function is to increase awareness and improve favourability. PR loses out to advertising in its controllability, but it has the advantage over advertising in its ability to communicate more complex messages and in its credibility. The press coverage achieved through media relations activity has the appearance of neutrality. Also the ability to target specific media and audiences is enhanced by the flexibility PR offers. For example, it is easier to target specific financial or governmental audiences through PR than it is through advertising. One of the oldest examples of effectively targeted public relations activity is the American Anti-Slavery Society. Formed in 1833 it established its own newspapers, held public meetings, distributed pamphlets and lobbied state legislatures and the US Congress, demanding action to abolish slavery. Even after the American Civil War the Society still campaigned for constitutional amendments and civil rights laws to protect the gains of the newly freed slaves. This led to the passing of the 13th Amendment abolishing slavery.

The limitation of PR, as with advertising, is the communication is one-way. Direct marketing is interactive: messages are not only sent outwards to consumers, but they are also received back. If companies choose to use this information – and many do not – then they can begin to understand more about their consumers and buyers and also start to build relationships with them based on an exchange of data. Some traditional mainstream advertisers, recognising the value of customer knowledge, have begun to shift their budgets into direct marketing activity. Partly this is a recognition that it is more important to maximise the loyalty and value of existing customers than pursuing the very costly exercise of customer acquisition. Partly it is a recognition that as markets become more competitive, those companies that are truly focused on delivering what customers want will succeed. Of course, it can be argued that through research, companies can understand their consumers and communicate with them by traditional advertising. This is true, but the differences are that direct marketing activity is more adapative and it is more focused. Also by acquiring knowledge about consumers, companies need not just be passive providers of products or services. In Don Peppers and Martha Rogers' book, *The One-to-One Future* they narrate the story of an independent florist,

> Last year a friend of ours on the East Coast called a local, independent florist in a small midwest city where his mother lived, to have flowers sent to her on her birthday. Three weeks before her birthday this year,

> he received a postcard from the same florist, reminding him (1) that his mother's birthday was coming up, (2) that he had sent spider lilies and freesias last year for a certain price, and (3) a phone call to the specified number would put another bouquet on his mother's doorstep on her birthday this year.[6]

Similarly, the video rental chain, Blockbuster, is now trying to use its database of 36 million customers and 2 million daily rentals to implement a computerised system that will recommend a list of ten film titles based on the individual customer's rental history.[7]

Direct activity is not limited to consumers. It works equally well in business-to-business markets and also in personal interaction. Companies regularly communicate on a personal basis with their key investors and with analysts to explain the scope of their business and their intentions, and they seek feedback. Sales forces interact continually with customers, gaining information. In pharmaceutical markets, speed and market knowledge are essential. Sales representatives call on physicians on a continual basis to inform them about new drugs and research. Through laptop computers and modems information is fed back by the representatives on a daily basis. As a consequence, information is built up and messages and targeting can be adapted.

The final part of the jigsaw in the communication mechanism puzzle is the use of visual identity. The identity will of course encompass the look of all the previously mentioned forms of communication, but it will also specifically include the company's logotype, typographic style, names, use of colours and visual imagery. These elements form the company's visual system and signals. The important point to recognise is that although these visual elements can be tremendously powerful and emotive – think of the visual system of the Nazi party for example – they cannot be treated independently of the company's performance. Is the Mercedes Benz symbol a good visual identity? Most people would say 'yes', but this is because we associate the symbol with the cars. In design terms, the symbol has an appealing simplicity and seems typically German – as does BMW and VW, but this hardly seems the point. The design of the visual identity can suggest a certain type of company or product, but once we experience the reality of the product, we tend to cease thinking about the identity as a separate element. This suggests that the prime concern for a visual identity should be appropriateness. 'Does the identity represent an accurate picture of the organisation?' is a better question than 'is it good?'.

Visual identity, PR, advertising, direct marketing and face-to-face interaction are the main ways in which an organisation sends messages about itself to the outside world. The conundrum for the communication strategist is how to decide the most effective way of determining and then managing the various means to market. One way is to work from the perspective of an organisation's audiences: to question what investors versus consumers versus suppliers need to know about the organisation, and when they need to know it. This helps to ensure that messages are always thought of in terms of the recipient. A communications strategy can then be evolved which specifies, within an overall positioning, the communication requirements for each specific audience. This should not encourage communication anarchy, with messages to shareholders contradicting those to consumers, but relevance. Working from audiences inwards also encourages an organisation to think of its communication mechanisms appropriately. Although television advertising might be a good way of exciting the interest of institutional shareholders in a company, it is probably not the most cost effective way, given that over 99% of the audience of any programme are not institutional investors. Of more value would be specifically targeted publications and especially briefing sessions and face-to-face presentations that help to move communication beyond the didactic to the interactive.

Summary

This chapter has tried to indicate the importance of integrating communications under one cohesive communications strategy that reflects the organisational identity. The communications strategy should be derived from the company's overall strategic stance and should reflect where the company is going – without becoming wishful thinking. To develop a strategy requires a full understanding of the organisation's various audiences and how to communicate with them. It should include all the relevant means, as well as the important, but often neglected resource of employees. This is the subject of the Chapter 6.

6 Employees and Communication

People are the corporate brand. They interact with audiences and each other, make the products that organisations sell and define and create marketing communication strategies. Perceptions of an organisation are determined, directly and indirectly, by managers and staff. It is their values and their idea of what the organisation stands for that give it cohesion and meaning. Yet it is surprising that employees are all too often ignored as corporate brand communicators by companies and their consultants. From a company perspective this is because, apart from those with overt communication roles, people are seen to be the responsibility of the human resources function. People tend to be regarded simply as a component of the organisation. Yet, look at any fledgling company and you realise that it is the people that define its existence. As organisations grow, the value of people can get lost amidst strategies and structures and finance, but the reality is that the management of people determines both competencies and strategies. The US retailer, Nordstrom, specifically derives its competitive advantage from the quality of its people. It achieves this not by training, but by selecting people that fit its ethos; people that have likeable personalities, good self-motivation and a willingness to serve customers. Employees are not indoctrinated into the Nordstrom way of doing things, rather they buy into the Nordstrom idea because it matches their personality and their vision of life. People enjoy considerable autonomy and are well rewarded: if the environment suits them they thrive, but if it does not they tend to leave. The system is self-selecting and self-perpetuating. The levels of service, derived from these people policies, is Nordstrom's key competence, which in turn leads to a strategy which seeks to nurture this point of difference. Nordstrom's policy is appealing and successful, yet it would not be appropriate to all retailers. The equally successful British retailer, Marks and Spencer, is much more oriented towards training and systems. People are not paid on commission as they are at Nordstrom, but by salaries. The service is good, but the defining competence of Marks and Spencer is the quality and value of its products. The key personnel within Marks and Spencer are the buyers, who work to clearly defined guidelines.

In both Nordstrom and Marks and Spencer, it is the people who define the nature of the corporate brand. To sustain the corporate brand, employees need to be able to perform their jobs functionally and they need to understand and be motivated by the higher aspirations of the company. Both are required and both need consistent and effective communication. This chapter will look at the some of the changing patterns of work and the implications this has for an holistic approach to employee communications.

Changing attitudes to work

Although on average the Japanese employee stays in one job for 14 years, the tendency in much of the developed world is towards mobility (in the UK the average length of tenure is 5 years and 6 months). This has come about for two fundamental reasons. First, the downsizing in both government and business in recent years, caused partly by the rapid development of information technology and partly by the credo of downsizing itself, as an effective means of boosting profits, has undermined the principle of employment stability. Companies no longer regard their employees as their long-term responsibility. There is an increasing use of out-sourcing in such areas as IT and clinical research and greater use of consultants to undertake project-based work. The world-wide value of business process out-sourcing contracts is expected to grow from $135 billion in 1996 to more than $280 billion in the year 2000.[1] Whereas companies like IBM used to have lifetime guarantees for their staff, these have been replaced by uncertain employment patterns. Second, in response to the lack of loyalty from organisations, employees have become disloyal. Charles Handy in his book *The Empty Raincoat* notes that 'Loyalty has to be reciprocal. Temporary contracts will beget temporary time horizons'.[2]

Managers tend not to see a job as a long-term affair, but something closer to a one-night stand. A job is where one develops one's skills, improves one's position and then moves on. This pattern is reflected by employees throughout the organisation. The example is set at the top and then replicated by the workforce. To overcome this infidelity, management and their employees have to be committed to a direction they both believe in and to each other. Only then can some kind of stability emerge. IBM's contracted employees are unlikely to share in the vision of the company if the relationship only lasts 6 months – it becomes just a job; an economic exchange without involvement. The economics of the situation may be rational, but any broader benefits are missing. In qualitative research conducted with contract employees in various roles, the same views emerge consistently: a sense of exclusion from the social aspects of the company; a lack of work relationships with permanent employees; a feeling of being second best. The absence of mutual commitment, contrasts with the policies of some of the companies previously mentioned, where there is a recognition of the implicit rights and duties of employers and employees. These organisations do not guarantee lifetime employment, but the reciprocity of the relationship helps to deliver a greater sense of loyalty. Here's the view of Leslie Wexner, Chairman of The Limited, the largest women's apparel retailer in the world,

> If your people believe you are providing fair, honest, consistent and intelligent leadership, they will be loyal to you. Leadership that is successful over a sustained period and is a demonstration of personal commitment will gain credibility. I believe true loyalty derives from the creation of good values, persistence in reinforcing those values, and the determination to communicate them.[3]

Connected to the emergence of contracts and job mobility is the trend towards virtual organisations. This movement has been facilitated by the desire of organisations to focus on core activities and shed peripheral ones and the emergence of IT. Following a long-held belief about the value of size and spread of risk, conglomerates were for many years very popular with business commentators in the UK and USA. Some cynics pointed out that unless a conglomerate's management could add value to its component parts it was only replicating what a shareholder could do. However, until the recession of the late 1980s and early 1990s, conglomerates were not really questioned at any fundamental level. Now analysts do question the remaining conglomerates; the vogue is for focus and concentrating on core activities. No longer does the corporate brand have to be stretched over a wide variety of activities; increasingly, it has to communicate only a narrow spread of business activities. However, this reductivism can lead to gaps. Whereas a company could once call upon a whole range of services within its corporate empire, it now has to look outside, or in some cases it can use ancillary services that are loosely linked to it: the virtual organisation. What the customer sees, or rather should see, is seamless service; a sense of the organisation providing a total offer. Behind the scenes, the scenario may be entirely different. The core of the organisational structure may only be a few people who set strategy and provide project management, while all other services such as research, production, marketing and sales are bought in. Charles Handy notes that organisations are becoming minimalist:

> The new shape of work will centre around small organisations, most of them in the service sector, with a small core of key people and a collection of stringers or portfolio workers in the space around the core.[4]

Similarly, Fukuyama states,

> it is possible to argue that in the future the optimal form of industrial organization will be neither small companies nor large ones but network structures that share the advantages of both. Networking organizations can take advantage of scale economies while avoiding the overhead and agency costs of large, centralized organizations.[5]

A good example of this flexible approach in practice is the pharmaceutical industry, who tend to contract out a whole range of services to others: early- and late-phase clinical research into a drug's efficacy, health economics studies, sales and marketing, advertising and health management. In spite of this, the buyer, whether they be a clinician or a patient, will not see anything other than a Bayer or a Glaxo Wellcome product. The core task for the companies, is to ensure that they maintain control over the processes done out of house and that they match their own standards: to maintain Johnson & Johnson's Credo (see Box 3.1, p. 39) requires careful selection of suppliers who will not compromise the company's deeply held beliefs. To ensure on-going cohesion requires a clear definition of the corporate brand and continuous two-way communication. As a consequence, most of the suppliers to the pharmaceutical industry have spent heavily on IT systems that provide instant feedback of results. The pharmaceutical industry is in the vanguard of the virtual company idea but, as the RSA, 'Tomorrow's Company' study notes, the concept is widespread:

> The trend is towards more work being done outside the traditional job box – often outside the company. As companies' boundaries become more permeable, they are forced to take a wider perspective on employment and work patterns.[6]

This blurring of traditional work patterns has also seen a change in the role of the office. Increasingly consultancies use 'hot desking' methods, whereby people simply take an available space when they are in the office. For the rest of the time, enabled by IT, they either work at their clients or at home. Nearly a quarter of companies now use home-based workers and 1 in 10 uses teleworkers. This change places a greater onus on the communication process. If individuals do not have direct contact with an office environment, they not only lose the socialisation aspect of work, they also fail to imbibe the culture that defines the corporate brand. Without lunchtime conversations, meetings at the photocopier, the exchange of ideas in meetings and the physical experience of the office, one cannot truly understand how an organisation works. For home-workers to identify with the company and its goals there needs to be an additional investment in communicating both the functional requirements of job performance and the essence of the organisation's beliefs.

Information technology has also transformed the nature of work. Sir Gavin Laird, General Secretary of the AEEU Union, noted in a 1995 lecture that by the year 2000 the UK will have an estimated 10.5 million managers and technical employees, compared with only 7 million manual workers – a reversal of the situation two decades ago.[7] This change means that due to automation fewer people are involved in the process of making and more people are involved in the process of providing customer service. It is the latter who will define the nature of the corporate brand in the eyes of consumers and determine the corporate image. This requires effective internal communication and the identification of employees with organisational goals: something that can only be achieved by committed employees over time. Identification cannot be instantaneous. Research by the management consultants, Bain and Company, demonstrates that where employees stay longer, so does the customer. And customer loyalty is one of the best predictors of profitability:

> The longer employees stay with the company, the more familiar they become with the business, the more they learn and the more valuable they can be. It is with employees that the customer builds a bond of trust and expectations, and when those people leave the bond is broken.[8]

Collectively, the changing patterns of work are decentralising authority, discouraging homogeneity and reducing loyalty. All these things make it harder to create a cohesive corporate brand. How do you encourage people to deliver consistent standards when you see them only occasionally and they feel little identification with the company? It suggests that organisations have to strive even harder to encourage interactive communication and to develop a unity of interest. Companies which achieve this can achieve substantial productivity gains. The author Kenichi Ohmae notes this unity is a feature of Japanese companies, because an employee 'feels married to the company for life and believes their fortunes will rise or fall together, he has in a way a top management perspective'. He later goes on to state that 'In Japan, the individual employee is utilised to the fullest extent of his or her creative and productive capacity.'[9]

This view is supported by research undertaken by the authors of 'The 100 Best Companies to Work for in America'. From discussions with employees they found some consistent traits which define the type of companies people favour. These were:

- they promote trust
- they empower employees
- they inspire pride.[10]

Effective employee communications

All organisations have either explicit or implicit rules and codes of conduct. An overt form of this was IBM's rules about dress – dark suits and white shirts – which its leader, Thomas J. Watson, claimed was a mark of respect for the customer, but had a strong militaristic tone. Similarly, Delta Airlines, having discovered that smiling stewardesses were a key asset, tried to regiment the process, so that employees, rather than smiling because they enjoyed their work, did so because they were told to. Whether dealing with dress codes or expressions of emotion, the attempt to codify what people do or look like requires communication. The problem that companies face is that individualism will continually strive to undermine the organisation's desire for conformity. In totalitarian societies it is possible to indoctrinate people into a certain way of thinking, especially if you repress alternative views, but in most organisations it is neither desirable nor achievable. Most companies are not truly democratic, but they do need to operate within a framework of legitimacy: a legitimacy conferred by employees. Decision making and communication must recognise this. Simon Ingman, Head of the Brand and Reputation Team at BT says that policing can only ever form part of the ideal of achieving consistency,

> You can't control communications throughout the organisation, you can only influence. You can cajole and you can reprimand, but that's post event. The only way is to try and ensure that people understand the direction and the strategy; you hope people buy into it and that they will be sensible and mature in their execution of it.[11]

Within the scope of communication there are two basic forms. One is instructive and informative, the other involving and empowering. Both have their place in the process of internal communications, but if there is a trend in modern organisations, it is away from the former and towards the latter. Instructive communications are an important way of ensuring systems are maintained and jobs done efficiently, but it is very difficult to tell people to be involved with what they are doing or to enjoy it. That can only come about through a sense of participation. As Duncan McGregor wrote in 1960 in explaining his theory Y – a more participative approach to management:

> Theory Y assumes that people will exercise self-direction and self-control in the achievement of organisational objectives to the degree that they are committed to those objectives. If that commitment is small, only a slight degree of self-direction and self-control will be likely, and a substantial amount of external influence will be necessary . . . Its underlying assumptions emphasize the capacity of human beings for self-control, and the consequent possibility of greater managerial reliance on other means of influence.[12]

The change that McGregor was beginning to notice and which has accelerated in recent years was a move away from traditional command and control structures. Partly this has become less viable as a means of management. The decline of deference generally in society, a willingness to question, a sense of greater mobility, general criticisms of managers' standards and greater access to company information through computerisation have all undermined the authority of those in power. The last has been especially noticeable. Before the advent of IT, information was strictly controllable on a need to know basis. Now with a personal computer on every office worker's desk, information is much harder to control. And as the adage says, 'knowledge is power'. Now it is far more difficult for managers to claim authority on the basis of knowledge. Partly the change has taken place because of most people's desire for more fulfilment from their working lives. The widely discussed notion of 'empowerment' is a result of this.

The idea of 'empowerment' is that employees at all levels of the organisation are to some degree responsible for their own actions and have authority to make decisions about their work. When operated successfully – in other words where the culture is supportive of a more participative style – empowerment has been shown to bring such benefits as:

- better customer service
- flexibility
- speed
- formation of important cross-functional links
- morale.[13]

It is a fallacy to assume that everyone wants to be empowered, for empowerment brings additional responsibility and stress but, as a general principle, loyalty, is more likely to be engendered when involvement and empowerment is a goal of communications. The problem with the principle is not so much whether it is good or bad, but that it is often difficult to implement: the culture has to be compatible and managers need the requisite skills:

> Empowerment cannot be decreed by top managers and 'rolled out' to the workforce. It cannot be bought from or introduced by consultants, although there are many who would try to sell it. Like the mutual trust that supports it, by its very nature empowerment must develop over a period of time, through the beliefs and attitudes of the participants.[14]

The example of ICI

The British chemical company, ICI, has been running an empowerment programme as part of a quality initiative since the mid-1980s. The thinking behind the programme was that it was becoming harder to gain competitive advantage through ever-increasing capital investment. To become 'world class', the company recognised the need to develop its people: to build a partnership with employees linked to higher productivity. Just as Toyota and other Japanese auto manufacturers have saved significant sums through competitions and employee suggestion schemes, ICI now use just such a device: in 1995, the company reckoned that employee ideas generated £120 million. However, this is just part of a comprehensive programme of involvement and motivation.

Commenting on the programme, Ian Griffiths in the *Independent on Sunday*, noted:

> In hard economic terms it is the single most important factor in determining ICI's profits and growth in the future . . . What empowerment has done is create a clear link between the customer and job security. It is a brutal but relevant truth. The benefits in terms of job satisfaction and customer satisfaction are tangible.
>
> One of the great attractions of ICI's empowerment is that it has aligned the interests of the workers with those of their bosses. That is in turn providing momentum for ICI to pursue its value opportunity programme. The intangible leads to the tangible.[15]

An internal communications model

Communications should be a simple process: it is about telling and listening. The complexity comes about because there are different ways of saying things and different ways of delivering messages. The following model (Figure 6.1) provides a method for looking at internal communications. The element which links communications together is an overall internal communications umbrella. This is derived from the unique identity of the organisation. For those who have experience of the organisation and have imbibed the values, some aspects of communication will become automatic. However, new entrants need to learn the communication protocols and acquire the necessary skills to apply them. The identity will define the unique set of organisational values and assumptions that determine the importance of internal communications to the organisation and how messages should be disseminated. If, for example, the culture has learned to value openness and honesty, then the protocols and training should reinforce these values. This leads to a virtuous circle, whereby the values of the organisation define the nature of communications, which when acted upon reinforce the values. As we saw with empowerment, communication protocols need a supportive culture. A communications planner may write a protocol that states, 'as an organisation we always be open and honest', but if the organisation has a history of being secretive (and has been successful with it) then change may be difficult to achieve. If being secretive has led to a disaster, this may be the catalyst for change, but it will undoubtedly take leadership and training and time for honesty and openness to become the norm.

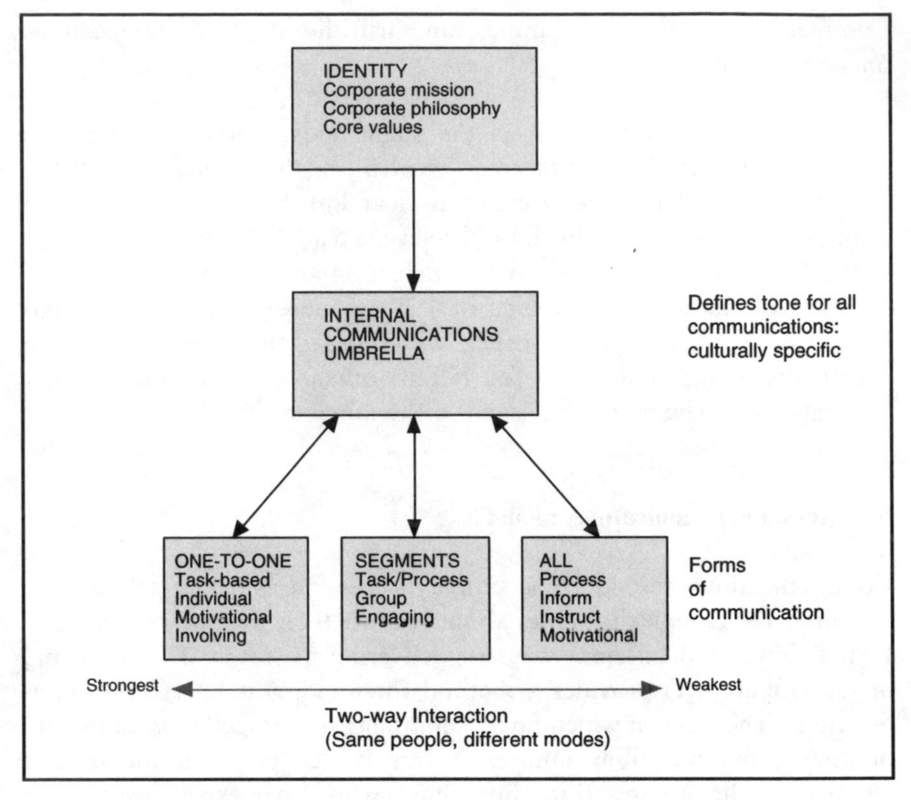

Figure 6.1 Internal communications model

The umbrella thus needs to take account of the organisational identity and its strategy. These should guide what is said to people. However, before we launch into an internal communications programme designed to transform people's behaviour, we should set some benchmarks. Qualitative and quantitative research should be employed to establish the way people currently think about the organisation, what they believe its values to be and how they judge its communications. Armed with this information, a programme can begin the process of informing and motivating through three basic forms of communication.

The first of these is communication with all employees. These tend to use internal mass media: newsletters, memos and brochures. Their primary role is to ensure that employees are informed about the organisation and its strategy. There is an element of motivation about these communications: people should be proud of the organisation and its performance – but direct motivation is easier to achieve through more precise forms of communication. Informational communications, no less than any other form, need to use a language and style that is consistent with the overall communications strategy. There is a tendency, because these communications are so everyday, not to pay much attention to look or content. Surely anyone can write a staff memo and do a presentation to the company? The reality is that these everyday things are often the least conscious of activities and can reveal people's deeper prejudices. It's the sort of situation where the well considered annual report tells the world that employees are empowered, while memos from the Managing Director keep defining rules and regulations. If the company is trying to convince everyone that empowerment is for real, the memos will undermine any credibility. The guardians of communication protocols need to watch for recalcitrant behaviour – especially from the managers who should be setting the example – while using focused training to help people be better communicators.

Within this all-employees' section is also the merchandising of external communications. Employees are likely to see external advertising or PR campaigns because they are also consumers and investors. Rather than just allowing employees to see these campaigns in the press or on television, it is valuable for the rationale and the execution to be previewed and explained to employees. People are more likely to support the tone and content of overt communications through their attitudes and actions, if they understand the meaning behind a campaign.

The second form of communication is to employee segments with common attributes. As with any external direct marketing activity, the idea with internal direct activity is to ensure that the right people get the right communications at the right time. All too often a piece of internal communication will be sent to all staff, when it is relevant only to a segment and perhaps demoralising to others. By analysing an organisation to discover the groups within it, communications can be more precisely tailored and consequently more effective. Using a grid which has a vertical listing of functional and/or psychological groups and a horizontal listing of countries or divisions, the defining attitudes and numbers of each segment can be plotted. This grid can provide a checklist for who should and who should not receive a piece of communication. For example, if a piece of communication only needs to be sent to a company's option holders, then the information can address the direct needs of that group, rather than having to be tempered by the knowledge that non-option holders will see it. In the range of information, segmented communication aimed at groups and teams has an information role, but it can, because of its precision, also be more involving and encouraging of interaction. Communication tailored to meet the aspirations of like-minded groups is more likely to generate a response than a generalised message. As long as this does not lead to the fragmentation of the core corporate brand, the relevance, and therefore responsiveness, can be increased. Of course, within this ideal one has to recognise that informal communications can undermine selective targeting and while focusing on specific groups the organisation has to recognise the impact of communications on other people not targeted specifically.

The third form of communication is one-to-one interactions. This type of communication tends to be task-based and, although it can be informative its primary role is involving and motivational. Within this form of communication is the daily interaction between people, such as between a manager and subordinate, as well as the more occasional reviews, briefings and meetings. This communication is very hard to control and continuity can be achieved only through strong and intuitive cultural norms that encourage people to think and act in a certain way. In organisations with strong values, this process can be self-sustaining: people who do not adhere to the organisational values simply find life uncomfortable and leave, while those people whose own set of values matches those of the organisation thrive and stay. In itself, this suggests the importance of psychological testing to ensure that the right people are hired. The more formal types of interaction can be more consistent, but only through the setting of communication standards that are acceptable to the organisational culture: if the organisation believes in openness as a central tenet, then setting a standard that says individuals should not discuss company performance with clients would be unhelpful. Setting communication protocols is only part of the process: for those protocols to have meaning, people need to be trained in the principles and leaders need to set an example by their actions. The ultimate objective should be for the standards to become part of the culture – unquestioned and unconscious.

Vertical and horizontal communication

Internal communications can move in three directions: downwards, upwards and across. Much of the communication just discussed is of the downward kind, although some of the more tailored mechanisms encourage upward flows. Such tools as performance reviews can be interactive both in the sense that they are consultative and because they can embrace both the manager's review of an employee and vice versa.

However, there are other ways of encouraging upward communication. Key to the process is a supportive environment. Processes such as employee involvement groups and suggestion boxes can deliver real benefits in terms of financial savings and improved productivity. But why should employees want to give their ideas? Sometimes there are financial inducements, but anecdotally the reasons seem more to do with identification with the organisation's goals and plaudits from one's colleagues and peers. Generally, the more directly related to an employee's specific role, the more effective the scheme. In a consultancy project for a recruitment group, there was a long-established employee suggestion scheme, which offered a significant financial reward for ideas. Although some employees were motivated by this, there were three barriers to its effectiveness:

- no one knew the sort of ideas required: was it about use of paper clips or suggestions on organisational structure?
- no feedback was provided on the ideas because it was too time consuming to do so.
- the ideas were not publicised widely and no one knew which suggestions had been implemented, and to what effect.

As a result of these limitations the suggestion scheme had largely become a cosmetic device, which suggested a notion of employee involvement rather than delivering it in reality. Suggestion schemes thus need to:

- be focused on corporate goals
- have the resources to evaluate and implement ideas
- keep the employee involved once the idea is accepted
- applaud good ideas and publicise the results.

A similar set of requirements applies to employee involvement groups. Japanese auto manufacturers are particularly good at achieving benefits through the use of teams focused on production improvements. A study by the Massachusetts Institute of Technology (MIT) found that the average Japanese auto plant is 119% more efficient than the average European plant. The interesting question here is: why? Ford and other mainstream manufacturers employ the same type of teams, but the reality is that companies such as Ford do not seem to have environments that encourage the same kind of effective team-based participation. This may be connected to the strong vertical elements in many European corporate structures: elements that do not encourage the effective transfer of skills or co-operation across divisions. In contrast Sony, like other Japanese organisations, places great importance on horizontal communications. Each year it has a Technology Exchange Convention, at which several thousand Sony employees come to swap ideas and spot opportunities. The company also uses committees and teams to encourage the cross-fertilisation of ideas. Teams, and especially cross-functional teams, can provide many benefits, especially in such areas as new product development.

> Team work has the additional advantage of making the group responsible for production decision. It generates peer pressure that helps enforce high levels of performance. There is substantial research showing positive effects of team-based work on reducing the need for management, increasing productivity and especially on achieving challenging goals that require creativity and problem-solving skills such as designing new products or developing new techniques.[16]

The importance of horizontal communications seems obvious: the basis of any multidimensional organisation is that it creates synergy. The different component parts of a organisation – if they are to have any validity – need to be able to communicate with and learn from each other. What Michael Porter calls 'inter-relationships' need to be nurtured:

> Strategically important inter-relationships have long been present in many diversified firms. Little attention has been given to identifying and exploiting them systematically, however, and many inter-relationships have remained untapped.[17]

In spite of the potential advantages, the basis of organisational loyalty is often narrowly defined. When career development and accountability are strictly vertical, with little horizontal movement, then the over-riding tendency will be to support the business unit or departmental view. This system is replicated in government. One minister, on first entering government was surprised at the power of the department: 'we came briefed by our departments to fight for our departmental budgets, not as Cabinet ministers with a Cabinet view'.

To try to build a broad rather than a narrow perspective of the corporate brand requires the organisation to recognise the benefits that can be gained from linking different parts of the organisation together. Employees benefit from a better understanding of the organisation as a whole and their place within it. It puts their work in context and enables them to see the value of their input in relation to the total organisation. For the employer, recognising the potential value of horizontal activity is sometimes an act of faith – especially in new product development. However, by deconstructing the organisation and comparing specific competencies with market opportunities new ideas can emerge. For example, Courtaulds' discovery of carbon fibre was the result of the combined knowledge of its fibres, polymers and weaving divisions, while the development of many Japanese products are the result of cross-organisational teams. What the Japanese seem particularly adept at is creating a direction from the swirl of ideas. To use a metaphor, Japanese organisations are more like a Jackson Pollock painting than a Mondrian:

> Japanese organizations, in which each function is loosely defined and each manager's area of responsibility slightly overlaps others, are typically much better placed to identify interface issues and act accordingly.[18]

The looser, less vertical structures found in Japan create greater opportunities for horizontal communication and the dissemination of what the corporate brand stands for than the rigidity evident in many European companies. In British companies, qualitative employee research into the pervasiveness of values and understanding of the scope of a business consistently show the failure of horizontal communications. To change the situation requires a change in attitude and structure and a commitment to fostering better horizontal understanding. To realise the benefit of inter-relationships, requires:

- A clear statement of organisational goals: a commitment by the parent to a defined and achievable direction, with regular feedback on progress made.
- The balancing of business unit interests with those of the parent: the most important values of the business unit need to be positioned alongside the interests of the parent. This may include individuals spending time on company-based activity rather than business unit projects.
- On-going, effective cross-organisational communications; not a one-off activity, but the regular communication of activity across the organisation.
- Demonstrating the benefits of inter-relationships to all employees: when there are successes derived from multifunctional teams the gains need to be celebrated.

Employees as customers

In an attempt to transform the relationship between employees and managers it is useful to think of employees as customers. Employees, like customers are knowing and cynical; they see communications for what they are. They recognise that companies inform and instruct them because they are trying to control their attitudes and behaviour. And like customers they look for the evidence of genuine intention behind advertising, literature and PR. Companies cannot fool customers and they can't fool employees. Once companies recognise their internal audience as mature and sophisticated they are less tempted to indulge in wish-based initiatives and concentrate instead on reality. Employees want to feel part of a successful organisation, but they also want to know about the challenges ahead and the company's strategy for meeting those challenges. Obviously the company should not be pessimistic about its future, but it should not be unrealistically optimistic. Finally just as customers can be activists for a company, so can employees. Customers and employees alike can become loyalists or even advocates. In fact employees start out with a greater pre-disposition to be positive – after all they have made a choice to work in an organisation. If the company can earn the employees' trust by being open and honest, people can easily become active supporters: demonstrating pride in their work, treating customers well and recommending the company to others. For this to happen, companies need to engage their employees at both rational and emotional levels:

> Traditionally, top level managers have tried to engage employees intellectually through the persuasive logic of strategic analyses. But clinically framed and contractually-based relationships do not inspire the extraordinary effort and sustained commitment required to deliver consistently superior performance. For that, companies need employees who care, who have a strong emotional link with the organisation.[19]

To achieve this identification – as with customers – the organisation has to ensure that the relationship is one of substance and dialogue. The substance should be derived from the organisation's clear commitment to strategic goals. The dialogue should be derived from communicating the goals in terms that employees can identify with – no vague aphorisms – and using the inputs of employees to help shape direction. Except in sensitive cases, companies should consult employees and seek feedback as they develop their plans. It helps to ensure ownership of an idea and provide support when the company makes a commitment to a given course of action. It also helps to ensure that employees have the necessary tools to implement a decision. If, for reasons of time or secrecy, the consultative process is not viable, then organisations should aim to inform employees of important decisions and their implications as soon as possible – even if the information is incomplete. There is nothing that demonstrates a lack of trust on the part of the organisation more readily than first reading about the company's actions in a newspaper. As an example of trust in action, take the biotechnology company, Celltech. In most companies the decisions of the Board of Directors tend to be closed affairs but at Celltech after every Board meeting there is a de-brief for any staff that want to attend – most do. The Board doesn't attempt to hide anything, either good or bad and staff are free to question the directors, even about sensitive issues. The result is an organisation where employees feel very much part of the organisation and where trust is pervasive.

The question remains: why is treating employees as consumers such a rarity? There are several possible answers. Companies are used to their command and control structures; the seeming democratisation of the workforce implied by dialogue can be a difficult step. Surely, they argue, managers are there to manage and employees to do. Second, consultation takes time – it involves listening to the ideas of many vested interests and then reconciling their needs. Third, it runs the risk of leaks of information to competitors and the press, thereby reducing the company's competitive advantage. Fourth, decision making gets watered down by trying to achieve compromises. Fifth, employees get diverted from what they should be doing. Sixth, difficult decisions such as closures or redundancy get postponed – because they affect the people being consulted.

All of these barriers have some credibility, but the reality is that in most Western societies people expect to have their views heard and to be involved in what they do. Companies can of course ignore the value of their employees and treat them as mere functionaries, there to perform a defined activity, but that wastes the creativity and ideas of all non-managerial staff. Nor does listening imply that managers should cease to manage; it means that managers have to re-think their role. In this framework management need to be able to harness and develop the skills of employees, to be good communicators and to nurture and manage good ideas. None of this is easy for managers brought up in a more traditional way of thinking, where lines of command are defined and expectations narrow, yet the benefits are clear. Bartlett and Ghoshal found after 5 years of research into 20 large, vigorous European, US and Japanese companies a consistent philosophy among their leaders:

> the objective is to change the relationship from one in which employees feel they work for a company to one in which they recognise they belong to an organisation . . . In the companies we studied that were best at achieving this new kind of relationship, top level managers focused on three activities. They recognised employees' contributions and treated them like valuable assets. They committed to maximizing opportunities for personal growth and development. And they ensured that everyone not only understood how his or her role fit[ted] into the company's organizational purpose but also how he or she might contribute personally to achieving it.[20]

The evolving organisation

This chapter has been devoted to looking at the role of the employee in enhancing the corporate brand. Key to the success of this is employee identification with the strategy of the organisation. This requires an empathy with organisational values so that there is a match between the individual's beliefs and the employer's. For example, an environmental activist would probably be more comfortable working for The Body Shop than an environmental cynic. But for employees to become true definers of competitive advantage they need to develop and adapt their skills to the benefit of themselves and the organisation. If one adheres to the view that it is the ability of individuals that differentiates one organisation from another, then it is axiomatic that the creative potential of people must be maximised. The way to achieve this is not primarily through 'top down' courses and training, but first by creating an atmosphere that encourages and stimulates learning. This is about taking a dialectic approach, akin to University learning, where within the parameters of a given area individuals can explore by themselves, or in teams, new processes and ideas. The atmosphere should be one of questioning; of always looking for a better way. This again suggests a tutorial role for management – something that the best Japanese managers are adept at. The principle behind this approach is that there is a far greater sense of commitment and participation if individuals discover things for themselves rather than being told how to do things. The second requirement for development is that individuals, in consultation, define their own training needs. This again is far removed from principles of scientific management but is close to the University learning model. All it requires is mutual trust: trust that the individual will choose courses appropriate to their role and trust that the organisation will provide an environment in which the individual can use their developing skill base. Training programmes that take little or no account of the organisational culture are unlikely to be beneficial to the company and will be frustrating for the individual. As an example of this, there is the famous case of International Harvester's foremen training programme. The company decided to try and change the attitudes and behaviour of its foremen by sending them to Chicago for 2 weeks for intensive classroom training. The programme was seen to be a success because there was a significant change in the attitudes of the foremen during the period. However, further research undertaken some time after the programme showed that the change in attitudes had disappeared and the foremen had reverted to type. The organisational environment simply wasn't conducive to sustaining the change the foremen had experienced in training.[21]

The potential benefit to the corporate brand of employee development is that consumers and other audiences will interact with better educated and more committed individuals. As well as improving the image of the organisation and providing the opportunity to develop consistent communications, employees can help the organisation to adapt to a changing environment and learn new ways of doing things. This process is now facilitated by the sharing of information through Intranet and e-mail. The Intranet – which uses the same structure as the Internet but restricts access to employees – is particularly useful for keeping international organisations informed. Ford have used the system to link its design centres in the USA, Europe and Asia in car development. The Intranet is valuable both as a horizontal and vertical communicator.

The perennial danger for management is becoming divorced from organisational reality. The traditional solution to this is to get out and wander about, to see the organisation at first hand and certainly some managers, such as Ingvar Kemperer of IKEA, have worked hard at getting to know people and customers. Now by combining computer-based tools with effective inter-personal horizontal and vertical communications the company can learn from its employees and adapt to changing circumstances. Arie de Geus' research into longevity – looking for those traits which enabled companies such as Shell, DuPont, Kodak, Mitsui and Sumitomo to survive a century or more – uncovered four key characteristics: conservatism in financing, sensitivity to the environment, a sense of cohesion and company identity among employees and tolerance. He describes the second of these, thus:

> The leaders of these companies were outward looking and part of their surrounding world. As a result, they were sensitive to changes and developments in that world. They saw early, concluded quickly; therefore, were able to take action quickly. These companies were mostly connected to their environment in ways which promote intelligence and learning.[22]

Of course the ability of individuals to learn does not necessarily translate into organisational learning. The organisation needs to devise ways to tap into individual knowledge and then to translate that knowledge into corporate memory. Sometimes companies make the same mistake more than once, simply because the implications of the error first time round are not absorbed. If the mechanisms are in place, the company will use the knowledge it gains from its people, either from their increased knowledge or direct contact with the environment, to question values and organisational norms. This should lead to corrective behaviour and the on-going evolution of the corporate brand as the new behaviour is 'tested' for its effectiveness. An example of this on-going learning was cited by Gregory Bateson in his book *Steps to an Ecology of Mind*, and is quoted by Argyris and Schon (see Box 6.1).

Summary

This chapter has been concerned with demonstrating how the attitudes and behaviour of employees is fundamental to defining the corporate brand. To achieve the cohesion necessary to differentiate one brand from another requires the organisation to build a committed and loyal workforce. The problem that many companies face is the continued diminution of loyalty. Partly this is of their own making and partly it is a reflection of changes in society. To develop a stronger relationship companies need to work harder at ensuring their communications flow upwards, downwards and across – tailoring the messages to the audience wherever possible and making sure that there is a compatibility of interest. This approach suggests that companies should recognise the talents of the individuals that work for them and that their skills should be nurtured through empowerment and learning.

Box 6.1 On-going learning

A female porpoise . . . is trained to accept the sound of the trainer's whistle as a 'secondary enforcement'. The whistle is expectably followed by food, and if she later repeats what she was doing when the whistle blew, she will expect again to hear the whistle and receive food.

The porpoise is now used by the trainers to demonstrate 'operant conditioning' to the public. When she enters the exhibition tank, she raises her head above the surface, hears the whistle and is fed . . .

But this pattern is [suitable] only for a single episode in the exhibition tank. She must break that pattern to deal with the *class* of such episodes. There is a larger context of contexts which will put her in the wrong . . .

When the porpoise comes on stage, she again raises her head. But she gets no whistle. The trainer waits for the next piece of conspicuous behaviour, likely a tail flip, which is a common expression of annoyance. This behaviour is then reinforced and repeated [by giving her food].

But the tail flip was, of course, not rewarded in the third performance.

Finally the porpoise learned to deal with the context of contexts – by offering a different or new piece of conspicuous behaviour whenever she came on stage.

Each time the porpoise learns to deal with a larger class of episodes, she learns about the previous contexts for learning.[23]

7 Communicating with Financial Audiences

The relationship a company enjoys with its bankers and shareholders is of fundamental importance. Their views of management, strategy and performance will help determine the company's ability to borrow money, its potential to acquire others and resist being bought and its share price. It seems therefore only rational that companies should attempt to influence the way they are seen, by keeping shareholders informed of their performance and direction. This applies equally to well known and lesser known companies. Research supports the idea that active and regular communication can deliver real benefits to a company's value. Charles Fombrun in his book, *Reputation*, notes that some analysts believe that the stock price 'of many diversified companies would probably be at least 20% higher if those companies helped investors make better sense out of the diversity in their portfolios'.[1] Similarly work by Higgins and Diffenbach shows that security analysts see a correlation between how effectively a company communicates its strategy with the valuation of a company's stock.[2]

In spite of the evidence that companies with an awareness of the need to communicate with financial audiences reap the benefits of an enhanced reputation and demand for shares, many underperform. The investment community sees this as a failing of corporate communicators. Investors are often critical of companies for their failure to deliver honest assessments of prospects and their fixation with short-term results. There is a view that many companies are good at communicating when there is something positive to say, but will avoid an issue such as declining industry margins until forced to confront it – either by the investment community or by the financial press. It seems that the problem most companies face is that communications with all other audiences tend to concentrate exclusively on good news. Advertising, direct marketing, PR are all concerned with partial honesty – with presenting the positive side of an argument. Breaking the habit when talking to financial audiences is hard, yet relationships with analysts, investors and journalists should be based on trust and openness. Misleading these audiences – either deliberately or inadvertently – is the worst sin a company can commit.

Companies tend to see the communication problem from a different viewpoint:

> Investors are perceived as placing a relatively low priority on the business fundamentals – such as customer loyalty, investment in people and supplier relationships – which will determine long-term success.[3]

The argument here is that investors seem only to be interested in the short-term profitability of an organisation not the core values and capabilities that make it successful. Many companies would argue that shareholders should benefit from sound strategies aimed at building employee loyalty and motivation and delivering customer benefits, rather than simply through the tactic of focusing on shareholder value. The real concern should be the long-term competitive advantage of the company. This view is supported by research conducted by investment bankers, Kleinwort Benson, who found that companies that adopt an inclusive approach – balancing the needs of various stakeholders in a non-adversarial way – outperformed the stock market as a whole during the period December 1992 and June 1996.[4]

In spite of the seeming logic of focusing on the business fundamentals, instances of investor short-termism surface with regularity, especially in the UK and USA. Even the much praised Marks and Spencer has suffered. On announcing good half-year figures for 1996, the share price fell 5% in one day. The main reason seemed to be that the company was planning to increase its staff by 2000 people to enhance the quality of its customer service. A sound strategic reason given the retailer's position and reputation in the marketplace, but disliked by the financial markets because of the additional cost. This is in spite of research by the Henley Centre for Forecasting, which calculates that bad customer service can cost a medium sized company £1.8 billion in revenues and £267 million in profits over 5 years. The research also found that a 1% cut in customer service problems could increase profits by £16 million over five years. A stronger argument for investing in customer service would be hard to find. David Potter of Psion also believes that financial audiences do not understand long-term perspectives. Citing the evidence of the IT industry he argues:

> I think real value in fund management comes from taking an independent view. You tend to find in the City that very few people beat the indices. In the late eighties everyone had to be in property and retailing – even when the shares were sky high . . . there is now a

> clamour of institutions wanting to buy in to us, whereas when we were a fifth of the price I was going round knocking on doors and they wouldn't see me.
>
> What I'm trying to argue against is the very short term cycles and fashions of the City. What they've begun to realise is that the biggest industry in the world – the IT industry – is being created under their noses and they haven't invested in this in the last 7 or 8 years in anything like the weight they should. American fund managers have and have done very well . . . 4 or 5 years ago we went through a poor patch, but we were actually laying down terrific foundations – they [the City] would have criticised us for being too strategic.[5]

The adversarial relationship that frequently exists between the company and its shareholders is in the end detrimental to both. This is partly a question of attitude, but it is also a function of the system in the UK and USA. In the UK companies are required to report their results to shareholders every 6 months and in the USA every quarter. Similarly fund managers have to report their performance to the pension funds they manage every 3 months. This reporting process, rather than just being an indicator of on-going performance, creates insecurity on all sides and encourages both sides to think of maximising short-term achievements and to distort decision making so that the timing of actions best fits their reporting calendar. A 1994 study by the Chartered Institute of Management Accountants found evidence that pension fund trustees do indeed use short-term performance figures to appoint and dismiss managers.[6]

The Anglo–American experience is not replicated in other parts of the world. In Germany and Japan the approach is longer-term. This is because in these two countries the banks have played a much larger role in economic development. Whereas companies in the UK and USA have funded their growth through equity offerings to institutions and individuals, in Germany and Japan the banks have been behind much of the funding. In Japan banks are often linked into the keiretsu, while in Germany banks were historically connected to specific industries such as the Berliner Handelsgesellschaft which helped develop the electrical equipment industry. The close and non-adversarial relationship between the company and its bank has led to bank representatives sitting on the boards of many major companies. The benefit has been a relationship built on trust where each party understands the other's interests and the bank is intimately involved with the success of the company. In his book, *Trust*, Francis Fukuyama notes:

Today these bank-centred groups (like their Japanese counterparts) provide a degree of stability in financing that permits German companies to take a longer-term perspective in their investments than American market equity-financed companies.[7]

Investors and the corporate brand

At a fundamental level investors are largely interested in the same corporate brand attributes as consumers. For this reason well known consumer brands attract attention among financial audiences. An investor in Marks and Spencer is interested in the quality of product that the company offers relative to its competitors and the company's reputation. Over and above this an investor is interested in very specific issues: past and potential performance, corporate strategy within a competitive marketplace and management capability. As with consumer audiences, an investor's understanding of the organisation will only be partial and will depend on the attitude of the organisation towards communication. Corporate history – from the South Sea Bubble to BCCI – is littered with shareholders with burned fingers, who discovered the truth about an organisation only when it was too late. To improve understanding and limit risk, shareholders try to acquire information about an existing or potential investment. This is easier for the institutional investor with research resources than the individual who has to rely on the interpretation of others. However, for a company that believes in the importance of corporate branding, the provision of information to investors should be an on-going and vital part of the communications process. If a company wants to earn the loyalty and support of shareholders it should aim to build a partnership based on trust with them.

How is this ideal to be achieved? Trust is the expectation that a company will act in an honest and co-operative way with its shareholders in line with established norms. Given that the shareholders are the owners of the business there shouldn't be any reservation about maintaining an open and free communication flow with them, yet as we have seen in the Anglo–American model a system of mutual distrust is common. Certainly overcoming short-termism is part of the solution: companies and shareholders need to take long-term perspectives; to look beyond the next half-year's results. The real solution, however, lies with companies and their willingness and ability to communicate. As with any other form of communication, the organisation needs to do it:

- regularly
- consistently
- appropriately.

Regularly

Because there are fixed points in a company's financial calendar, the temptation is to think of communications only at these times. However, a once-a-year flurry is of little benefit. Under the auspices of senior management, communication should be seen as a continuous task in which the company focuses on telling its investors its long-term plans, providing performance data and seeking feedback. This helps to present a clear picture of the business and reduces the risk of surprises.

Consistently

Investor communications should present a clear picture of the organisation and its strategy. Communications should not be tactical, but rather they should reflect the positioning of the organisation both in terms of content and tone. Consistency also applies to a unity between financial communications and those with other audiences. Consumer advertising should not be sending out one idea of the company, while financial PR sends out another. The information emphasis may be different, but investors shouldn't be confused about the organisation's purpose.

Appropriately

If companies want investors to focus on the long rather than the short term, then communications should concentrate on the former. The tendency is for companies to bemoan short-termism and then focus on immediate results and actions. Companies also need to be as open as they can in providing an insight into the true nature of a business and its prospects.

Means of communication

Organisations have various communication means open to them to convey performance, strategy and management quality. These include managed mechanisms such as press relations, advertising and the annual report as well as more direct forms, such as presentations and interviews where there is the potential for a greater degree of interaction. The private investor tends to rely much more heavily on the managed mechanisms than the informed investor who has greater access to the people who run a company. Research into the information sources for informed investors[8] helps define the relevance of sources (see Table 7.1).

Not surprisingly the direct relationship between financial audiences and the company is seen to be the most important source of information. This view is supported by qualitative research which shows that professional investors are influenced primarily through direct dialogue with company chairmen, finance directors and other board members. It is only through contact with these senior businessmen that investors believe they can form a true picture of a company and its long-term prospects:

> Institutional investors look to City analysts for guidance on how they view a company, yet they have a mind of their own. So their thoughts are formed most firmly by relationships with executives of companies in which they have an interest.[9]

The dialogue between directors and investors should be exactly that: a candid and on-going two-way conversation. For company directors, it helps in understanding the expectations of their financial audiences. For investors, it provides first-hand experience of the organisation's management – especially important where there is a dominant figure running the company – and the ability to probe any areas where in-depth information is required. Companies that try to delegate this communication process to consultants tend to come in for criticism, simply because the filtering takes away the interaction. As with other areas of a company's activity, it

Table 7.1 Mean importance ranking of financial information sources

Sources of information	*Investment analysts*	*Institutional investors*	*Combined*
Preliminary profit announcement	1.27	2.50	1.89
Personal interviews	1.48	1.67	1.58 (1)
Interim statements	1.48	2.90	2.19
Company presentations	1.57	1.92	1.75 (3)
Annual report	1.62	1.67	1.65 (2)
Telephone conversations	2.10	2.67	2.39

SOURCE: D. Bence, K. Hapeshi and R. Hussey, 'Examining Investment Information Sources for Sophisticated Investors Using Cluster Analysis', *Accounting and Business Research*, 26(1) (1995), pp. 19–26.

is the 'people aspect' that matters; the building of trust between directors and investors. Rather than adversarial thinking, there should be a commonality of interest – a joint desire to maximise the long-term success of the company.

In addition to the obvious information about strategy and performance what, if anything, should the company be telling its investors? Some would argue for an inclusive approach:

> Mr Sheehan [a Kleinwort Benson fund manager] insists this more rounded approach is indicative of the way the City is going. Earnings per share is no longer the key measure it was . . . Investors and researchers are more intent on finding out the sources of value.
>
> Furthermore just as environmental issues are now taken seriously, it is not inconceivable that analysts will see the value of loyal customers and keen employees. After all there is no point making perfect products if staff don't bother to answer the phone.[10]

There is a feeling that factors other than the numbers are exerting an increasing influence on analyst perceptions. Opinions still vary as to whether the numbers or such issues as customer loyalty are more important, but there does seem to be a broader analytical perspective. Similarly analysts and investors cannot help but be swayed by the direct experience of the companies they look at. Flying with British Airways or drinking Coca-Cola or seeing Nike advertising influences investor opinions of these companies, either by confirming existing ideas or by raising doubts.

Environmentalism is also treated more seriously by many organisations. Of the FT top 100 companies, 65 reported on the environment in their 1994 annual reports and 34 of them produced separate environmental reports. Go back 10 years and environmental policy was hardly an issue and certainly not a publicly stated one. Partly the change is a reflection of public opinion and partly it is due to the wide range of pressures exerted upon the corporate brand. In their study of environmental reporting, KPMG note the following factors:

- banks require information on the financial implications of environmental issues
- financiers and shareholders need to evaluate how environmental regulations may impact on sales and cash flow
- employees and shareholders need to be reassured that companies are acting responsibly towards the environment

- environmental groups, the media and the public may be concerned about the potential damage to the environment or to health
- customers are increasingly concerned about the implications for their own operations and reputation of poor environmental performance by their suppliers
- the growing number of standards on environmental reporting is exerting pressure on companies to report on their environmental performance.[11]

Collectively these factors demonstrate that companies cannot pigeonhole communications. The pressures exerted come from a wide variety of sources and several audiences take note of corporate performance other than those for whom the information is specifically intended. This is less true of the direct interaction between directors and investors, but occurs all the time through less controlled circulations, such as media comment, advertising, literature and the annual report.

Corporate advertising

The use of corporate advertising to enhance awareness and status is rarely aimed purely at institutional investors who dominate the shareholding of British and American companies. If it were it wouldn't be a very cost effective device. Corporate advertisers are trying to influence the perceptions of individual shareholders, influencers, lobby groups, suppliers, bankers and consumers. This is of particular importance if the company is a potential acquirer or acquiree. If it is the former, it will not only have to influence its own shareholders, but those of the target company and possibly legislators. If it is the latter, then it will help retain the loyalty of existing shareholders in the face of a threat. When the conglomerate Hanson embarked on a well known advertising campaign in the mid-1980s under the banner of 'a company from over here [UK] that's doing rather well over there [USA]', it had a series of objectives:

- to generate a sense of employee pride in the company's achievements
- to retain the loyalty of existing shareholders (in spite of being 70% owned by a few institutions, the company had 125 000 shareholders on its register)
- to communicate Hanson's strategy to key influencers
- to communicate Hanson's achievements to consumers.

The important aspect of this communication process is that it needs to be an on-going commitment. Corporate brands take time to build and there is very little benefit in throwing money at trying to build awareness only when the company is about to conduct a takeover or ward off a threat. Most of a corporate brand's key audiences are sophisticated and will recognise a knee-jerk campaign for what it is.

Annual reports

The arguments relating to corporate advertising also concern that key influencer, the annual report. The sums expended on the writing, design and print of annual reports is huge and in the largest companies an all-year-round activity. No sooner has one annual report been mailed than work starts on the next. However, in spite of the quality of design of some reports there is a tendency towards sameness in the tone of the reporting. There appears to be an innate conservatism of approach and a blandness to many reports. The report should be delivering three core messages: historical performance, an insight into the company's future and an indication of management capability. It should also deliver information on – where relevant – the performance of divisions, geographical spread, environmental stance, employee policies, products and services and financial data. However, all of these should be delivered within the context of the corporate brand. The annual report should be a unique reflection of a unique organisation, not simply a parody of the style of others. Therefore it should integrate – while delivering specific messages – with all of a company's other communications. The barriers to achieving this are the focus on a perceived narrow idea of audience (shareholders) who first and foremost should see the company as professional and the devolving of responsibility of producing the report to people (company secretaries, financial directors) who are different to those responsible for other forms of corporate communication. As a consequence, annual reports can end up being ambiguous communicators of the corporate brand. As an example, a company's claim to be truly concerned with its employees is sometimes flatly contradicted by the tone of the annual report – a very negative situation if the company has a large number of employee shareholders. Cohesion here, as elsewhere, is a matter of management and belief.

Changing perceptions of the corporate brand

Institutional investors are the dominant force in the UK and USA. For example, not only do they account for 90% of all transactions on the New York Stock Exchange and 60% of all stock held, they also influence the actions of individual shareholders. Given this hold over the marketplace the question arises: how can companies change the attitudes of investors towards a corporate brand? The important factors are to do with performance and management. Investors react positively to companies who deliver what they say they are going to do and who seem to be able to manage a company so that it is clearly and effectively positioned in the marketplace. This suggests that changing attitudes cannot be an overnight transformation – a sudden appreciation of hidden talents or potential – but rather an experiential change proven over time. If a company is a poor performer it cannot change this simply by improving the quality of its communication. However, paying attention to communicating can yield two benefits:

- Qualitative research suggests that analysts and investors see the quality of communication as an indication of the overall quality of management. In other words, good managers are good communicators.
- Complex organisations can be reappraised if the way they communicate is reworked to make the organisation more relevant or comprehensible. In this case, a good performer can have its reputation boosted by paying more attention to communications. This factor is also linked to the idea of equating quality of management and communications. Communication is thus a signalling device, which has validity if the signal turns out to have credibility.

Signalling

One of the key ways that an organisation can signal that it is changing or has changed is through a change of name or visual identity. This process is undertaken with some frequency in the USA, where communicating with financial audiences assumes a greater importance than in the UK. There is some evidence that name changes do provide benefits. In a study of some 355 name changes over 23 years, the researchers determined:

> The most important finding in our study is that we are now convinced that name change does have an effect on stock price. We also believe,

however, that the type of name change is important, rather than just the name change in general.[12]

Positive name changes are attributed to the following:

- adoption of acronym
- adoption of initials
- adoption of personal name
- adding name of merger partner/acquisition
- removal of limiting descriptor
- replacement of initials
- simple truncation
- verbal escalation

Negative effects were found to be rare, but the following occurred:

- adoption of a brand name
- adoption of an acquirer's name
- change to description

While some changes seemed to have little effect:

- change of description
- legal status change
- newly devised name
- rollback of earlier name change.[13]

However as the researchers themselves recognise, 'association does not guarantee causality'. The research leaves unresolved the dilemma of why name changes have an impact. However, as noted, UK research indicates that name change is often part of a wider intent and it is this that is valued rather than the name change *per se*. The opinion of UK financial audiences concerning the mid-1980s' change of Woolworth plc to Kingfisher plc was that by itself it had no impact on perception. Similarly, the US-based airline operator, United Airlines, changed its name to UAL as it diversified into car rental (Hertz) and hotels (Hilton and Westin) and then again to Allegis, as it continued its expansion into non-airline areas. Whether the financial community was judging the strategy or the quality of communication as an indication of the strategy, the Allegis name was not a success and there was a rapid reversion to UAL. As Neil Harlan of the foods and distribution company, McKesson once recognised, investors understand all too well the reality of corporate performance:

> We used to do an annual survey of the opinions of investment analysts about the company. It always came out the same: very few positive comments for the simple reason that the company wasn't doing very well and hadn't done well for four or five years. We were regarded as a kind of sleepy, old, dull company with lacklustre performance, because that's exactly what we were.[14]

Should one conclude therefore that Tampax's change to Tambrands or ICI's claim to be 'world class' or Consolidated Foods transformation into Sara Lee are at best inconclusive and at worst a waste of money? Although there are problems of cause and effect again, some of the evidence suggests that, provided the company can support the signal, there can be real benefits. For example, Consolidated Foods, in adopting the name of its best known brand, Sara Lee, boosted its awareness from 93% to 100% among US security analysts, from 82% to 97% among portfolio managers and from 79% to 100% among the media. In the 18 months following the change of name the stock price nearly doubled. But then food stocks during this period generally did well. And the name change was made to increase awareness of restructuring and its resultant benefits in terms of sales and income. Could this have been achieved without a change of name? Possibly, but a name change supported by marketing communications seems to have been significant in boosting awareness – something one imagines would have been harder to achieve with the name Consolidated Foods.

Similarly, Bausch and Lomb, the manufacturers of Ray-Ban, always found they were categorised and tracked by a small band of analysts in the manufacturing sector. Given their development as a service-based healthcare company, management felt their status was inappropriate. To correct the situation the company began presenting itself as a service company with four divisions: personal health, medical, biomedical and optics. The real benefit of this was that management found it easier to articulate what the company was and where it was going. Different analysts started to track the company and the stock price rose significantly following the representation. Again one cannot claim causality, but performance in itself has no importance in a financial market unless the investment community are aware of that performance. Investors will try to gain that information and companies should aim to provide it in a way they consider to be relevant and beneficial. As with all other aspects of the corporate brand, communication here should be about building a relationship.

Fighting for attention in a crowded market applies equally to consumers and investors. Well known organisations, such as Sara Lee and Bausch and Lomb, by virtue of their size, importance and opportunity to communicate will tend to be noticed. Smaller companies or new corporate brands need to stand out if they are to create interest in their shares. When a new company decides to float its capabilities and potential will be fighting for attention alongside other companies. Whether potential investors notice them will depend on how well they present their case. In this context, communications and forecasts need to be credible and well argued. The company needs to use its direct presentations, PR activity and literature in a coherent way to communicate its essence. Although the process of communication is informative rather then overtly persuasive, the company needs to use the power of design and language to stand out and create a tone that is an accurate reflection of the organisation and its strategy. This suggests that the forms of communication used in this market will be individual, but as with annual reports the perceived success of established formulas and conservatism tends to createc a sameness to most documents and presentations.

Occasionally a need for stand out impacts on a large organisation. The Japanese car and truck manufacturer, Nissan, had marketed its cars in Europe and the USA under the name of Datsun since the early 1960s. As the company grew the existence of two brand names began to limit the company's ability to market itself globally and to market its stock in the USA. Nissan felt that if there was a clear link between its cars and the parent company through a common name, analysts and investors would take more notice. In 1981, the company changed its name to Nissan, but the problem the company faced in spite of an extensive advertising campaign was the resilience of the Datsun name. Longer-term, the decision probably made sense, but in the shorter term the exercise was costly and potentially counter-productive as it created confusion about the Nissan brand.

The Nissan story contains an important lesson – not the least of which is get your branding policy right in the first place – in that as companies seek listings on a multinational basis they need to recognise that the awareness of the corporate brand is unlikely to be as strong as in their home territory. A German or British company that decides to promote share ownership in the USA will have to build awareness of its brand to achieve that goal. When the conglomerate Hanson wanted to promote share ownership in the form of American Depository Receipts (ADRs) and create the idea that it was a successful US corporation it had to build awareness through advertising and PR in the financial press and an active investor relations policy. In the space of a year US ownership of Hanson had risen from virtually nothing to 20%. Invariably overseas companies need to work harder than indigenous organisations. This may be because their products are not available in a country or because they do not have a manufacturing/office presence of any note or because they are culturally distinctive in approach and attitude. All of these barriers may need to be overcome to achieve the sort of profile that will stimulate and then maintain interest among investors.

Summary

Shareholders and their influencers are rarely seen as the primary audience of an organisation. Most would argue that shareholders benefit from a company focusing on its customers and employees. In spite of this, companies should invest time and money in building strong relationships with investors and analysts. Problems occur because of a lack of unity and understanding. Companies believe that investors are obsessed with short-term gains while investors think companies don't communicate often or well enough. Both sides need to understand the perspective of the other. There is a suspicion that the lack of trust between the company and its shareholders means that companies sometimes communicate the bare minimum of information, somewhat grudgingly, while investors are only too willing to look for short-term gain because they don't have faith in the information they acquire. If there were greater openness and trust then both parties might be more willing to improve the quality of communication. Also staying in for the long term often provides the best return for the investor. The problem of getting the timing right has been demonstrated by Peter Bernstein in his book, *Against the Gods* – a history of the way risk analysis has influenced the markets.[15] He points out that if during a 14 year period, an investor switched out of US equities into cash for just 5 of the best trading days, they would have doubled their money. However, if the investor has simply stayed in the market through the highs and lows of the 3500 days they would have trebled their investment. The real-life case of this is the fund management arm of the Union Bank of Switzerland, PDFM, which in predicting a fall (which happened) switched some equity into cash, too early, and found themselves at the bottom of the performance league tables.[16]

The as yet unsolved mystery of financial communications is how the process of signalling works. Companies, especially in the USA, do embark on communication or identity programmes with the specific intent of influencing their share price, yet institutional investors, who dominate the market in the USA and UK, claim not to be heavily influenced by these communications. They claim their primary source of information is through a direct interaction with a company's management. However, the judgements of financial audiences, as with any other, are not uniform – especially as they are concerned with trying to speculate about future performance. Each investor has a unique view and will interpret the information they receive from their own perspective and experience.

8 Mergers, De-mergers and Strategic Alliances

In most coherent organisations, there is some sense of identity and strategic direction. People may not be able to articulate it and it may be blurred by a business unit identity, but there is normally some glue that holds everyone together in the pursuit of a common purpose. In quite large organisations there is normally an accepted way of doing things: a set of cultural precedents that people can draw on. All of this, however, can become unravelled when the status of a company changes. When an organisation merges, de-merges or allies itself with another, questions about what the corporate brand means for both internal and external audiences start to be asked. There is uncertainty and fear and a lack of understanding as to what the new relationship with the organisation will be. Its values and purpose may change – factors that perhaps had determined the reason for the relationship in the first place. Its strategy may alter and change the business rationale for being a stakeholder. At worst, the company may cease to be a friend and become an enemy.

Why do it?

All forms of mergers and alliances are high risk. They involve putting one unique set of values together with another in the hope they will meld. Not surprisingly in acquisitions, it is most often the acquiring partner that is marked down by the investment community, not the acquired. Cultures will be difficult to gel, management will need to spend time to make the acquisition work, most likely there will be redundancies and morale of the workforce in the transient period will suffer. The reason why organisations and individuals put themselves through this highly stressful process is the need to gain competitive advantage:

> Acquisitions provide a way to broaden a firm's scope through adding positions in new segments, positions in new geographic areas, greater integration, or a beachhead in a new related industry . . . Acquisitions

> can also play a key role in re-configuration or pure spending strategies. Acquisitions can allow two organisations to combine resources and skills in such a way that reconfiguration or pure spending is possible.
>
> Coalitions also bring together skills and resources of firms in ways that allow reconfiguration, redefinition or pure spending . . . the coalition that led to Airbus Industries has made a world-class competitor out of a group of struggling national firms.[1]

Building an international organisation or developing a new competency is a lengthy process through organic growth. Through mergers and alliances, the process can be achieved rapidly. Attaining the scope to compete in some industries is well-nigh impossible without partners – witness Airbus Industries and the group that created the Advanced Photographic System. Ann McDonagh Bengtsson, who researched the motivations of acquisitors, found the following reasons:

- exploit synergies
- increase market share
- market protection
- product acquisition
- strengthen core business
- gain footholds abroad
- achieve critical mass-competitive size.[2]

Research by the strategy consultancy, Braxton Associates, into 800 alliances formed during the 1980s presents the key alliance drivers in a different way:

- globalisation
- change – either technological or political
- risk reduction.[3]

Braxton also found that companies enter into different sort of alliances for different reasons, such that gaining market share is more valid for undertaking an acquisition, while risk diversification and geographical expansion are two key reasons for entering into a joint venture (Figures 8.1 and 8.2).[4] An interesting judgement from the research is that there are benefits in alliances: by comparing the performance of the *Fortune* 500 with the 25 companies most active in alliances during a 4-year period, Braxton found that the average return was 50% higher for the alliance activists. But, 'while the returns were up by about 50%, risk also went up

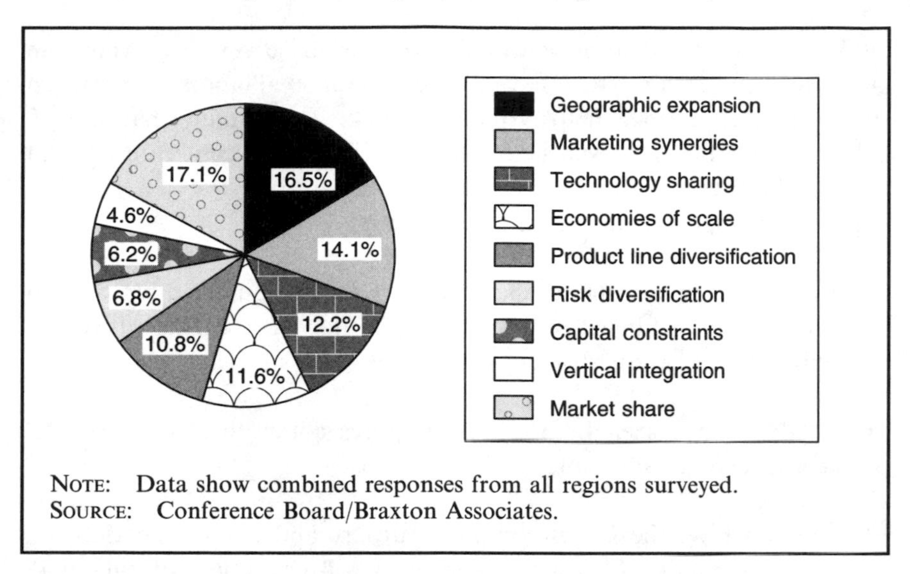

NOTE: Data show combined responses from all regions surveyed.
SOURCE: Conference Board/Braxton Associates.

Figure 8.1 The goals of strategic partnerships

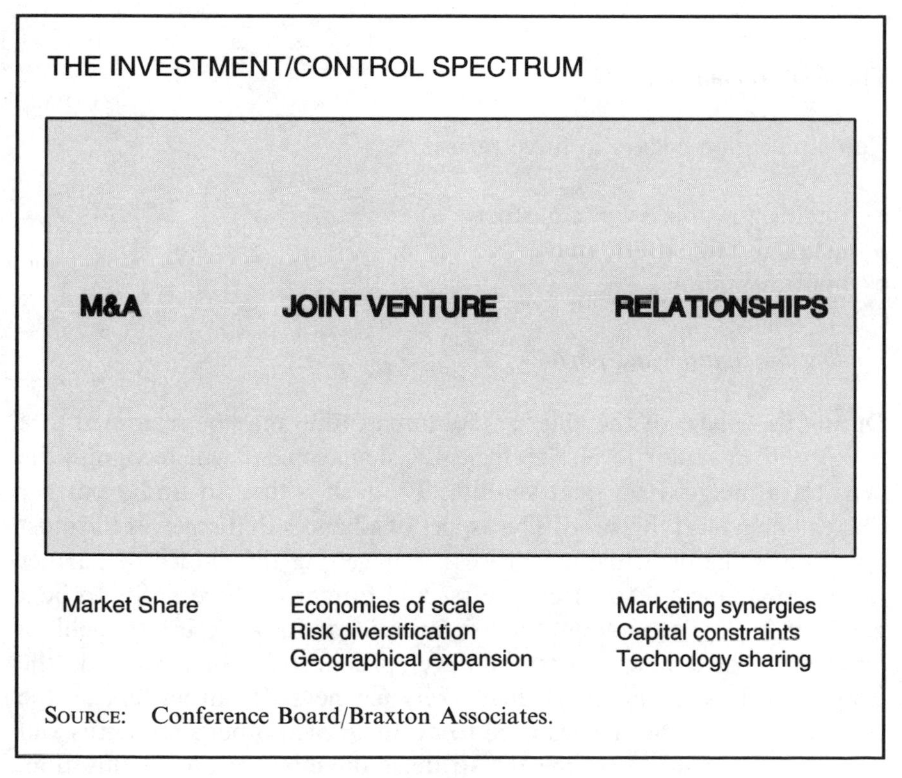

SOURCE: Conference Board/Braxton Associates.

Figure 8.2 The investment/control spectrum

by 50%'.[5] For serial joint venturers, such as the diversified American manufacturer, Corning, who have formed about 50 alliances over the last 70+ years, experience helps to reduce risk. They claim that only 9 alliances have failed – 'well below the "over 50" per cent rate of joint venture failures in general'. Corning believe that the single most important component in their success rate is

> Trust . . . an environment, an attitude, a specific guide to action that requires a genuine belief in the integrity of the other partner. It means avoiding excessive questioning and doubt.[6]

Trust, as we have seen before, also requires communication. As Joel Bleeke and David Ernst note:

> in relationships, the key is common purpose and communication . . . the most carefully designed relationship will crumble without good, frequent communication.[7]

The need to communicate

Communication occurs in three phases:

- finding the appropriate partner
- managing the interregnum
- implementation.

Finding the appropriate partner

During this phase of the alliance, communication may be restricted to a few people at senior level. Strategically, management will recognise the need for a merger or a joint venture. The task is then to find a partner that will help meet this need. The aspect of alliances that receives the most attention is the deal making process, but getting the choice of partner right is fundamental to success. First and foremost, there needs to be a good strategic fit between the organisations. In a desire to achieve penetration of a new market or develop a new product, there is the temptation to seize upon the first likely partner. Yet all writers on the subject stress that both sides need to evaluate each other's strengths and weaknesses and to determine the strategic direction of an organisation.

This process should also involve investigating reputation. Does the organisation have a good track record in alliances? Have they proven themselves to be trustworthy in the past? Do they have hidden agendas? One of the danger areas, especially in joint ventures is the sharing of technology. One partner could be obtaining short-term market access, but in the longer term creating a powerful competitor. There was certainly an element of this in the joint venture between Honda and Rover. Rover improved its working processes and technological capability hugely through its alliance with Honda. Honda, for its part, gained better access to the lucrative European market. However, with the acquisition of Rover, the capabilities Rover developed during the alliance now benefit BMW. One of the distinct features of joint ventures is that they need trust to make them work, but unlike an acquisition they tend not to be forever.

In acquisitions, given the need for secrecy, investigating the cultural fit in anything but a perfunctory way can be difficult. The acquiring company has to rely on what it can glean from published reports, the tone and style of its communications and from asking people who have had previous experience of the company. The acquirer should be seeking to unearth the type of people that work for the company, the systems and methods used to manage the company and its values and strategies. This will be easier for a well defined corporate brand, such as Nike or Johnson & Johnson, than for an organisation with a low public profile and ill defined values. As was observed in Chapter 1, the problem is the intangibility of most corporate brands from the outside. The danger here is that limited knowledge can lead to a mistaken perception of the target company's culture which will be truly discovered only when the acquisition goes through. In this situation it is important for the acquirer to recognise the partial nature of their judgement and to remember later on that the cultural fit analysis was incomplete. The risk is that a cultural myth will become fact unless more work is undertaken after the acquisition is complete. The second phase of the fit exercise is proper self-appraisal. Again assumptions can be dangerous, but unless this phase is undertaken with reasonable objectivity – probably by an outside consultant – judgements about potential conflicts will be missed. Citing three examples of failed alliances, the writer Edgar Schein notes:

> What is striking in each of these cases is the lack of insight on the part of the acquiring company into its own organizational culture, its own unconscious assumptions about how a business should be run.[8]

If the perceived cultural incompatibility is such that the acquisition is likely to be impaired, then the acquirer should be prepared to say 'no' and walk away from the deal – no matter how much loss of face this costs. Mergers and acquisitions are an emotional (and expensive) experience, especially if they are contested, so maintaining objectivity can be difficult. With one in two takeovers failing, more caution should be exercised in the early phase. Sorting out a problem purchase will be both time consuming and costly.

Given the uniqueness of corporate culture, the reality of any proposed venture is that there will be points of cultural dissimilarity. As Corning suggests, the search should be for the common values that will help two companies integrate.[9] If the values are antithetical, the union is unlikely to work. With variances of a less profound nature, the judgement will have to be made as to whether they can be managed cost effectively. It is almost inevitable that there will be differences in international acquisitions. The very nature of national cultural assumptions determines distinct views on such areas as management control, status and time scales. This is particularly noticeable in many European alliances:

> Reports of culture clashes within European cross-border partnerships are not uncommon; for example, the *Financial Times* (1991) has attributed declining performance of the Metal Box–Carnaud merger to conflicts between the autocratic management style of the French and the more participative orientation of the British. The partnership between GEC and Siemens was reported to be marked by contrasts between the British firm's decentralised and short-term approach and the centralised longer-term style of the German partner (*Financial Times*, 1990).[10]

Due to the less secret nature of strategic joint ventures and the opportunity for greater openness, it is easier to conduct an authoritative evaluation of the cultural fit at an early stage. This should involve looking at the points of difference and determining how they will be managed when the venture is under way. Adopting 'role reversal' techniques is a useful way of getting the partners to think through how they might work together and to appreciate each other's perspectives. Rosabeth Moss Kanter equates this phase of a joint venture to courtship: when both sides learn more about each other and test out their assumptions. In the case of a joint venture the partners can also indulge in some premarital coupling. Citing the successful collaboration of the advertising agencies FCB and Publicis, she notes:

The FCB-Publicis alliance is evidence that, especially in fast moving industries, potential partners must find compatibility in legacy, philosophy and desires, because specific opportunities are often short-lived and won't sustain a long-term relationship. A relationship that falters or fails as soon as the first project is concluded precludes other opportunities from developing.[11]

Managing the interregnum

Once a partner or target is identified there will be a period of uncertainty as the deal is put together. This will be a difficult time for all parties. Senior management have to devote their time to the alliance process, while still trying to manage the business on a day-to-day basis. Employees will be uncertain about the implications for their jobs – should they leave now, hang on for the redundancy payment or wait to see whether their position is enhanced. Suppliers and buyers will be unsure if this means a change in their relationship. Everyone is uncomfortable. In merged companies it is common to find falling productivity, rising staff turnover and poor employee morale. These are difficult factors to overcome. Some companies, such as Unisys – created by the merger of Sperry Univac and Burroughs – used employee merger psychologists to help overcome 'signs of trouble'. Referring to these signs, the psychologists Mitchell Marks and Philip Mirvis state:

> While they occur to some extent in nearly all corporate combinations, our experience shows that they can be limited and managed effectively with the help of psychological knowledge and techniques.[12]

Much of the psychologist's work is in getting both sides in the alliance to understand each other's perspectives. This can be a hard task if the new partner has long been presented as the devil incarnate to the company's employees, but is a necessary process in turning an enemy into an ally.

During this coming together phase, there are three key requirements to maintain the progress of the alliance:

- *Clarity*: It is important that the alliance is explicit about its purpose. Both sides need to be clear about what they hope to get out of the deal and to root out any hidden agendas. Responsibilities and management structure need to be clearly defined, the likely brand structure needs to be agreed and in the case of a joint venture, the scope and duration of the arrangement needs to be determined. This does not deny the possibility of evolution after the deal is consummated, but at least everyone knows where they are starting from. For example, when Matra approached Renault with the idea for a people-carrying van aimed at the European market in 1983, Renault agreed to the idea on the proviso that the vehicle should be constructed such that it could easily be transformed into a commercial van, if the people-carrier concept didn't work. For Matra, the Espace was to be a core element of its work, whereas Renault saw the product as a small-scale niche project. In the end, not only did the Espace create an automotive category it became something more than small scale. The original idea of the alliance had to evolve from Renault lending its brand weight to the product to a more active involvement in production processes and quality control.

- *Communication*: Implicit in the need for clarity is the requirement to communicate decisions both internally and externally. There may, of course, be some constraints about what the organisation can say in the period between when the deal is announced and ratified by shareholders, but over-communication is preferable to under-communication. Ann McDonagh Bengtsson says that 'employees of companies conscientiously kept involved and up to date were prouder of and more loyal to the new organisation than those left in the dark.[13] Rosabeth Moss Kanter found in her analysis of 37 alliances that companies tended to underestimate the need for communication.[14] All of an organisation's audiences will want to know how the alliance impacts on them – in the absence of any communication people will make their own assumptions. Whereas company newsletters and memorandums may be scanned or ignored by employees and others, during normal working times, during the development of an alliance, everyone will be desperate for communication. Suddenly newsletters will be pored over and memos reread for hints of what is happening. Speculation will be rife, people will be drawing up their own versions of likely outcomes and informal communication will assume significant importance – especially if the source is seen to come from the top (or near to it) of the organisational hierarchy. The onus on management therefore is to maintain continuity in communication through specifically targeted and carefully worded messages.
- *Speed*: In their attempts to retain the culture and people of the acquired or merged company, the acquisitor often slows down the pace of integration. This is particularly noticeable with people-based

businesses, where there is often an attempt to preserve the acquired corporate brand for at least a period of transition, such as with the combining of the Dutch bank ABN-AMRO with the British company, Hoare Govett or UBS and Phillips & Drew. Others such as Glaxo Wellcome and Pharmacia and Upjohn have retained the dual brand, but gone for rapid integration. The advantage of the fast approach is that financial benefits are achieved more quickly and the momentum for the merger is maintained. Allowing the merged companies to drift along without any attempt to integrate tends to encourage people to notice the differences, rather than the similarities. However, if the rationale for acquisition is the desire to acquire people skills and brand reputations, the merger team needs to be sensitive to the corporate culture and work on the process of integration. This inevitably slows the process down and can extend the period of uncertainty: internal and external audiences will be looking for the longer-term hidden agendas.

Implementation

Although alliances can fail because of faulty logic and poor planning, commentators on alliances are almost universal in their agreement that the most difficult area is in implementation. A study by McKinsey & Co. of 49 cross-border alliances found that two-thirds of them ran into serious trouble within the first two years. The authors of the study, Joel Bleeke and David Ernst note that 'alliances by their nature are laden with tensions . . . these inherent tensions require more flexibility on the part of the parents than many other business strategies.'[15] During this phase of the alliance, the organisation has to go public on what it is, what it intends to do, and how it is going to get there. Uncertainty has to be resolved. Whether the alliance is a joint venture or a merger, a new corporate brand will emerge. Ideally it will combine the best attributes of the partners and provide value to its stakeholders. More often it will be something of a curate's egg, with the optimal solution arrived at only over time. Understanding relative strengths and weaknesses, especially in the emotional atmosphere of an acquisition, is never easy. It requires the management of the respective parties to be impartial about the best way forward – often, while fighting to retain their jobs. Most mergers simply do not need two marketing directors or two financial directors, although some shuffling of the pack can help retain key staff, there are almost certainly going to be some discards. In successful alliances management challenge each other and develop new and better ways of working, while one of the key process failures of alliances is poor integration.

Sometimes an alliance will retain an existing corporate brand name or names, but the process of allying will affect the fundamentals that define the corporate brand: history, management, strategies, products, communication, processes and values. For example, the alliance between Aérospatiale, Daimler-Benz, British Aerospace and CASA to form Airbus created a new entity. Although the organisation draws its senior personnel from the operating companies and is influenced by their cultures, it has a specific identity of its own determined by its leaders, technology, shared knowledge, strategies and focus on a common external enemy – Boeing. In the case of Unisys, committees were set up to develop the company's operating procedures. The committees were briefed to find a new way of doing things, that was neither Sperry Univac nor Burroughs, but rather distinctively Unisys. The project required the committees to achieve cost savings of between 20% and 30% and to appoint someone to head up each area. The result was a new corporate brand, built from the ground up.

The 1996 merger between two giants in clinical research, Quintiles and Innovex, has led to a restructuring of the group into three divisions. Although there is reasonable autonomy within the divisions, the success of the merger will depend on the degree of organisational learning: what can each party learn from the other in the development of a new corporate brand. This will require a structure that encourages horizontal communication and the rotation of people. In a joint venture the danger is that the organisational learning can be locked into the alliance itself and the parent companies fail to reap all the benefits. This was the case with Chrysler and Mitsubishi who had to build a rotating management structure to ensure skills were unlocked and passed to both partners:

> Each partner contributes three members of the joint venture's six member board and decisions are taken by unanimity. Design and engineering had to be staffed up through a complicated and time consuming interlocking of Chrysler and Mitsubishi personnel.[16]

In a joint venture, implementation is made more difficult by schizophrenia. The personnel who make up the joint venture have loyalties to their parent organisation and its strategies and to the joint venture itself. This tension is evident within Airbus. The senior personnel may be directors of Airbus, but the President is also a director of Aérospatiale, the CEO is a director of Daimler-Benz and the Finance

Director is a director of British Aerospace. This inevitably creates conflicts. It is important that although the parent companies actively support the joint venture, it also has a staff and an identity of its own – BAeSEMA is an excellent example of this. When the situation is a merger, loyalty has to be engendered by the new entity. Retention of loyalty to the previous component parts will prevent integration. As noted before, loyalty cannot be imposed, rather it has to be earned. Through integration teams, employees need to be involved in the process of helping to define what the new organisation stands for. This requires trust and a belief in the importance of communication. Management need to communicate the rationale for the merger to all staff and to explain its implications. Horizontal communications need to be encouraged through cross-organisational groups and job rotation and upward communication needs to be promoted, so that people feel they have a stake in the new organisation. Finally, management need to resolve the branding issue.

Branding

The approach to branding needs to be considered in the context of the strength of the existing brands, the closeness of the alliance and the strategic direction of the new entity. When the existing brand identities are strong the tendency is to retain existing names, such that the alliance between British Aerospace and SEMA is known as BAeSEMA and the merger between SmithKline and Beecham is known as SmithKline Beecham. The advantage this approach enjoys is that the value of the respective corporate brands is retained. This is valuable if the partners both have strong corporate brand reputations or have specific reputations in distinct business areas. It is a question of evaluating the relative corporate brand strengths from each stakeholder group's perspective to establish the best scenario, and then judging this in the light of strategic intention. If, for example, two corporate brands have powerful reputations in their own markets, this might suggest the retention of both names, but if the long-term plan is to build a business primarily in one of those markets it may be best to concentrate on developing one brand name. In the short term it is easier, quicker and less confrontational to simply put two names together, which avoids the demotivating signal – especially to one part of the internal audience – of dropping one corporate brand. However, retaining the name of both partners is not without problems. It can:

- be convoluted – witness the extraordinary length of the names of some advertising agencies
- help sustain the separateness of the two organisations and signal the lack of integration to audiences
- be problematical for global organisations if they wish to develop a world-wide brand under a different name to that of a local merger.

So the system may work well for SmithKline Beecham, but it is difficult to imagine Airbus being called 'Aérospatiale, Daimler-Benz, British Aerospace, CASA'. This would be difficult to say and communicate and encourage division, when unity is required to compete against the mighty Boeing.

Creating new identities or subsuming one name into another is not without difficulty. It does help establish a clear and communicable brand identity that people can understand, but it will require investment to help get across the name and importantly the corporate values and it may hinder business in the short term. A new name suggests a new way of doing things while the disappearance of onc name probably suggests to most audiences that the operating practices and culture of the disappeared brand have been replaced by the dominant name. This can be unsettling to external buyers and suppliers who will need to be told how their business relationship will change and to employees, who are left in no doubt who the dominant partner is. The rationale of a new name for Unisys, rather than retaining either Sperry or Burroughs, was that the Chief Executive didn't want people to feel either victors or vanquished.

In analysing the impact of any new brand name, consideration has to be given to the influence this is likely to have on the image of the parties. What does the acquirer brand name add to the acquiree, and vice versa? Will it enhance reputation or undermine it? And what will any new corporate brand name add to products? In the case of Renault–Matra's Espace, the consumer branding is Renault. Matra has missed out on the opportunity to establish its own brand credentials, but it is Renault's corporate brand and back up that has helped to ensure the success of the vehicle – something Matra would have struggled to achieve with its more limited resources. Similarly when the acquirer is Nestlé and the acquiree Rowntree, then the reputation of Nestlé adds value to consumer products and helps create unified branding of products in a number of countries. Although Rowntree had a good national reputation it was the company's brands such as Kitkat that were recognised by consumers. Kitkat is now endorsed, along with other Rowntree products with the internationally powerful Nestlé brand.

If the alliance is a joint venture, the problem of branding and communications can be more complex. As well as retaining the communications strategy and brand of the venture partners, the venture itself will often need to be branded. The question here is how will the reputation of the parent impact on the joint venture, and vice versa? And how will it be managed? To avoid the problem of schizophrenia, the venture entity can have its own marketing and communication team, but this carries the risk that joint venture communications can start to run counter to the positioning of the main brand. The important point is that the parents of the venture are clear in their own communication strategies – from the outset of the alliance – and have a real influence over the activities of the joint venture. To succeed the venture needs freedom, but that freedom has to be in the context of the venture serving the needs of the parents' strategies.

Often it is the sorting out of the visual identities that resolves the above issues. Should the joint venture dominate the parents' identities in communication? Should the visual identity of one partner simply be hitched onto the other, as BT does by retaining its piper graphic for its European joint ventures or have a new name and identity as BT does in its Concert alliance with the American telecoms company MCI? In judging the logic of naming and brands, alliance members are forced to confront the meaning behind the visual. What may seem appropriate when discussed initially may seem illogical when it is communicated to the outside world.

Communicating externally

Once the rationale for the alliance has been agreed and communicated internally and people understand its implications, the new corporate brand should be launched externally. It is important that internal buy-in is achieved, because whereas in normal circumstances stakeholders may accept marketing communications without question, in the context of an alliance everything will be carefully scrutinized. Shareholders who might not normally query a decision to change the location of head office or move directors around will now be looking to see whether these moves indicate any change in the relative strength of the partners or strategic direction. Similarly, once an alliance goes public, suppliers and buyers will be asking employees, about the implications for them. Employees cannot constantly refer back these issues – they need to be fully briefed and supportive of the corporate intent.

Those charged with devising corporate communications need to be aware that what they produce will be carefully monitored. The tone of language, the relative position and size of logos, pre-eminence given to an advertising style will all send signals about the relationship between the alliance partners. The external campaign needs to be credible and sustainable for both internal and external audiences. Employees will be looking at the external messages intently for sub-texts to check whether advertising and literature is consonant with what they have been told by management. If having reassured employees there will be no redundancies, press comment suggests that management anticipate the alliance will lead to cost reductions of 30%, people may start questioning how this will be achieved. During the limbo period between announcement of intent and launch there is likely to have been a lack of external communication. Management will argue there is little point in promoting a corporate brand if it might not be around in 3 months' time. Or that there is no point in producing sales literature until it is clear how the alliance is to be named and presented. Into the communication vacuum rumour will pour. Commentators may judge that a company is going to withdraw from a particular sector or scrap its sales force. Employees, shareholders, competitors, suppliers and buyers will all be speculating on what is likely to happen and be drawing up plans accordingly. The task then for the companies involved in the alliance is to act as fast as possible – a difficult task in the context of management over-work and differing perspectives on communication. Advertising, newsletters, press releases, presentations and briefings need to be planned and co-ordinated. All audiences – many of whom will inevitably be sceptical – need to be informed, if the business is not to be tarnished and market share lost to aggressive competitors. During this time more than any other the alliance partners need support – something they can earn only from past performance and active communication.

Once external promotion of the alliance has begun it needs to be supported over time. This not only helps to build up a coherent image of the organisation, it is also reassuring to all audiences. When it has taken perhaps 30 or 40 years to establish a corporate brand, a new version cannot be created overnight. With established goodwill, the process can be rapid but it cannot be instantaneous. The in-built advantage that the strong corporate brand possesses is that it will have created interest through entering an alliance. People will approach the new brand with interest in a desire to see if it is still the same or whether it has changed in some way. This point also indicates the importance of monitoring progress. Given the potential impact on morale of an alliance and the need to demonstrate the benefits of the venture as soon as possible, tracking the opinion shifts of employees, shareholders and all other audiences needs to be integrated into the communication plan. If the alliance is to be a success, the development and communication of a new corporate brand is fundamental, but as with any brand there will need to be evolution and adaptation. This can only be achieved by listening and learning – two attributes which should be core to all alliances.

Summary

Alliances are an important fact of corporate strategy and research demonstrates that CEOs regard alliances as likely to grow in importance. This is not surprising given the need to save time, share risk and technology and to compete effectively in global markets. There has also been a shift away from diversity and towards focus. Companies are now more pared down and need joint ventures to offer services that previously they might have undertaken themselves. With more emphasis on alliances, there is increased pressure on choosing the right partner and managing the integration process. This should involve investigating the cultural fit, as well as the financial and strategic need in a partnership. Incompatible cultures will make the process of integration that much harder and more time consuming – this can be especially difficult in international alliances.

Once partners have committed to an alliance, the rationale and the benefits need to be conveyed to employees and subsequently to external audiences. Part of the process of coming together should involve an assessment of branding policy – establishing how the component elements should be put together and what each adds to the other. Forming an alliance is a time for excitement, but also of danger: 50% of alliances fail and in most cases there will be redundancies, but there are also opportunities to forge a new corporate brand and build new competitive advantages.

9 The Global Brand

> If as a competitor you are not convinced about global presence, then you should consider that your domestic market competitors are more likely than ever to be global companies. That means you are engaged in global competition even if you are sitting in Dubuque and are perfectly content to have Iowa as your market.[1]

There are a number of well documented forces driving the globalisation of competition in established markets:

- a more open approach to trade
- the globalisation of consumer tastes
- demographic convergence
- a willingness to accept products and ideas from other countries
- access to information
- potential for achieving economies of scale

which means that local companies in Dubuque, even if their horizons do stretch no further than Iowa, will have to face up to the implications of competition from companies that have a national and international presence. This fact has implications both for the Dubuque and the global corporate brand. The local brand will not only have to consider its competencies relative to its immediate competitors, but also relative to the global brand. If, for example, it is in document delivery, how does it compete against the might of such competitors as UPS and Federal Express? Probably it needs to hone its service quality based on specific local knowledge. Equally, how do UPS and Federal Express, compete against this local knowledge? Probably by stressing the benefits of consistent service and global reach, underpinned by the reassurance of a well recognised brand name. In this unequal encounter in terms of resources, both sides possess competencies that they need to emphasise. The error that either side could make is to confuse the nature of competition. There is room for both to win, but only as long as the local competitor recognises the nature of its niche and positions itself accordingly and as long as UPS and Federal Express do not have to radically rework their systems and branding to be effective locally – this would undermine the rationale for global branding and probably be uneconomic. Companies need to be global competitors and insiders. This factor is at the heart of the issue of global branding. From one perspective, global brands can only be truly global if they are significantly the same in most of their markets. This requires recognition of the source of an organisation's global advantage and the management of global strategies and structures. If the recipe and bottle design of Coca-Cola changed in every market in which it operated then the company would lose the benefits of global marketing and economies of scale. Similarly if British Airways offered highly variable levels of service in different parts of the world, then its claim to be a global brand with a global strategy would lack foundation. Consumers and other stakeholders – especially those who experience a brand in different parts of the world – need to be reassured that the company and its products are essentially the same and adhere to the same values everywhere in the world. In spite of the need for consistency, the other perspective is that local adaptation is fundamental to success: global brands still need to compete in Dubuque. For example, McDonald's maintain their principles of quality, service, cleanliness and value, everywhere in the world. There is a global vision about how things should be done and the training and marketing resources to support it, yet there is a significant degree of local adaptation to the food it serves,

> In its 2,700 restaurants outside of the United States, McDonald's carefully customizes its menu and service to local tastes and customs. It serves corn soup and teriaki burgers in Japan, pasta salads in Rome and wine and live piano music with its McNuggets in Paris.[2]

The automotive world's search for the nirvana of the world car is similar. Ford have been struggling for years to produce a car that can be sold throughout the world and may have only just achieved the breakthrough with the Mondeo. Chrysler are attempting the same with the Neon but have had to adapt the suspension for European markets because of the nature of the road system. American cars have traditionally had soft suspensions because the prevalence of highway driving means straight line comfort has been more important than rigidity in turns. Europe, with a higher incidence of minor roads with a larger number of turns, requires cars that are comfortable going round corners. The nature of the road systems will therefore continue to dictate either adaptation or compromise of a global product. The problem,

Chrysler has to face in the short term is its lack of image in the UK. There is probably only a vague recognition of the company as an American producer and the status of its cars, which means that a corporate image needs to be established as well as the car's virtues. Europeans know how they feel about driving around in a Renault or an Opel and they know the status it confers. For the time being the signals emanating from Chrysler are few. The problem for Chrysler and others like it, is that there are forces encouraging homogenisation and forces encouraging heterogenisation. Organisations have to structure their corporate brand to meet these opposing forces.

Opposing forces

The political scientist, Samuel Huntington, has argued that cultures are becoming more distinct; that people in Teheran do think and act differently to people in Beijing and people in New York.

> As indigenisation spreads and the appeal of western culture fades, the central problem in relations between the west and the rest is the gap between the west's efforts to promote western culture as the universal culture and its declining ability to do so.[3]

Even the arch proponent of universal liberal democracy, Francis Fukuyama recognises that nationalism is increasing at least in those parts of the world which enjoy 'relatively low levels of socio-economic development'.[4] However, whereas Huntington sees divergence as a long-term trend as people seek to define their own values independent of western culture, Fukuyama sees nationalism as a merely transitory phase in the path to global liberal democracy:

> Nationalism continues to be more intense in the Third World, Eastern Europe and the Soviet Union and will persist there for a longer time than in Europe or America. The vividness of these new nationalisms seems to have persuaded many people in developed liberal democracies that nationalism is the hallmark of our age, without noticing its slow decline at home . . . Economic forces encouraged nationalism by replacing class with national barriers and created centralized, linguistically homogeneous entities in the process. Those same economic forces are now encouraging the breakdown of national barriers through the creation of a single integrated world market.[5]

A more balanced view is that there is a simultaneous divergence and convergence. Just as the power of the European Union grows, so smaller – and some larger – countries express stronger feelings of nationalism. While McDonald's thrives in Moscow, extreme nationalism in Russia is a powerful unifier. While the Malaysian government has built a car industry as a symbol of national pride, it also encourages foreign direct investment. Nationalism with its sense of uniqueness and togetherness has a popular emotive appeal: people from all types of backgrounds were enthusiastic supporters of the British government's decision to invade the Falklands in the early 1980s and the 'Falklands Factor' has been widely attributed as one of the key reasons for Mrs Thatcher's re-election in 1983. Yet rationally, the reasons for the war and its benefits are much harder to justify. As well as finding pride in national feeling, many people also like to express their cosmopolitan side – an awareness of and interest in things foreign. This is expressed through travel, entertainment and consumption.

Convergence

Even if ideas about human rights, women's rights, environmentalism, democracy and free markets, so cherished by most of the West, do not enjoy the same interpretation and value in other parts of the world, business and brands seem to be converging globally. There are three core factors behind this movement, which is most noticeable in the developed world:

- demographics
- cross border trade
- media

Demographics

Demographically there are trends that have implications for many international brands. Throughout Western Europe the number of households is rising as the average number of occupants per household declines. This is due to a significant rise in the number of one-person households all over Europe and the fall in the birth rate, with the attendant rise in the average age of the population. One of the key causes of the decline in the birth rate, below replacement level in much of Europe and Japan, is the change in expectations and consequently, careers of women. In the USA the influx of immigrants and the higher than average birth rates of ethnic minorities means that the birth rate remains above replacement level.

What implications do these common trends have for brands? They provide the opportunity for products and services to market themselves not to national segments, but to similarly structured international segments. Home security, furnishings, entertainment and food are just some of the products affected by single-occupancy households. An ageing population places consistent demands on healthcare generally and specifically in such areas as indigestion, arthritis and rheumatism. A pharmaceutical brand in any of these areas will find itself with a global customer base. Similarly Glaxo Wellcome's ulcer treatment, Zantac, has become the best selling drug in the history of the pharmaceutical industry because of the need for such a product throughout the developed world. Marks and Spencer is in the process of defining itself as a global brand, because of the appeal it has for a generally upmarket and older audience. The 50–75 year age group account for 55% of all Marks and Spencer grocery shoppers, 49% of all its spirit buyers and 35% of its wine buyers. Interestingly this age group also accounts for 47% of all Toyota Carina car purchases.[6]

Trade

The various economic and political groupings that came into being during the Cold War – the OECD, Group of Seven, European Community and GATT – have all been concerned with the promulgation of the principles of free trade. Occasional protectionist moves, such as the attempts by the French to curtail the tide of Japanese car imports or American Republicans attempts to stem Far Eastern and European infiltration of the American economy, have been largely side-shows. Protection, such as it does exist, does so within trading blocs. The European Community provides advantages to EC member countries – something the Japanese have recognised by building up their manufacturing capacity within EC member states, most notably the UK. As a consequence of this activity intra-Community trade has become dominant for its members over the last 15 years and accounted for nearly 62% of exports in 1992. The retail trade, which has long been a national bastion, is also becoming internationalised. Companies such as The Body Shop, Marks and Spencer, Benetton, The Gap and Disney are all now international retail brands. The ability of consumers to purchase these products at similarly competitive rates in different countries has helped drive the development of these retailers as global brands.

The globalisation of trade is also mirrored in the globalisation of finance. Companies increasingly seek listings on various stock exchanges, use advanced treasury systems to channel money around the world to take advantage of interest rates and exchange variances and seek finance from banks across the world. The global brand not surprisingly adopts a global financial perspective and the world's financiers in turn have been moving rapidly to develop their own global structures.

Media

Estimates of global Internet usage vary, but anything between 25 and 40 million people now have access to the Internet. This world-wide phenomenon not only helps to convey information to people, thereby encouraging a convergence of attitudes, it also provides huge marketing opportunities for the global communicator. Similarly through cable and satellite a whole raft of specifically targeted communication opportunities have become available – everything from MTV to CNN to The Children's Channel. All of these channels are defined not by nationality, but by commonality of interest. In the print medium, such publications as *The Economist*, *Cosmopolitan* and *Time* reach global audiences interested in a specific area.

Divergence

Globally fragmented brands

Although the evidence is towards increasing convergence of lifestyles across the developed world, the opposing force is divergence. People increasingly want to express their individuality and companies are meeting this by seeking to build relationships with their stakeholders. This leads to fragmentation of global brands – they cease to be universal except in a few core ways and become more adaptive. This runs directly counter to earlier principles of global branding, where the thinking was to achieve the maximum economies of scale by the minimum degree of adaptation. In many markets, this approach is no longer sustainable. Consumers expect both local and global companies to listen to their needs and then act upon them. In many markets this means going beyond the mere provision of a product to providing retail service support, contact with consumers, after-sales back-up and adaptation of features –

the same sort of service a local competitor would provide. For example, research conducted by the Henley Centre for Forecasting into consumer attitudes shows that interaction with friendly and experienced staff and the provision of manufacturer information are the improvements consumers would most like to see in such areas as cars and personal care products.[7] The debate here for the global brand is how to control the process of downstream service. The answer lies in devolving power down to the local level as far as possible, but maintaining consistency through training and the setting of global standards – the solution offered by globally adaptive brands such as Andersen Consulting and McDonald's, who place great emphasis on common values and a standardised process, reinforced by thorough training procedures. Companies without this approach have to work that much harder to achieve consistency. Companies that do not control the relationship with the consumer because they do not have sufficient power over distribution channels can also suffer from variable corporate image. This applies equally to car manufacturers who do not own their own dealerships as well as computer manufacturers whose products are sold with minimal advice from warehouse outlets.

Divergent nationalities

The second point of divergence applies especially to non-consumer audiences.One of the observations of Jack Benfield Wood, who runs executive programmes at IMD in Switzerland, is that while participants in his programmes initially associate on the basis of nationality, once they begin to know each other the affiliations become based on other factors.

> In essence, the executives affiliate with those who look at the world the way they do, or who have a similar, shall we say, management style. In other words, these participants affiliate with others who have the same set of beliefs as they do or who have a similar character. The configuration of individuals and subgroups within the seminars are not defined exclusively by – or even predominantly by – culture but by ideology and personality. It seems to me that ideology and personality run 'across' national culture and tend to form dimensions along which individuals from different cultural backgrounds coalesce.[8]

Wood uses a matrix (Figure 9.1) to describe the inter-relationship between culture, ideology and personality across five countries: USA,

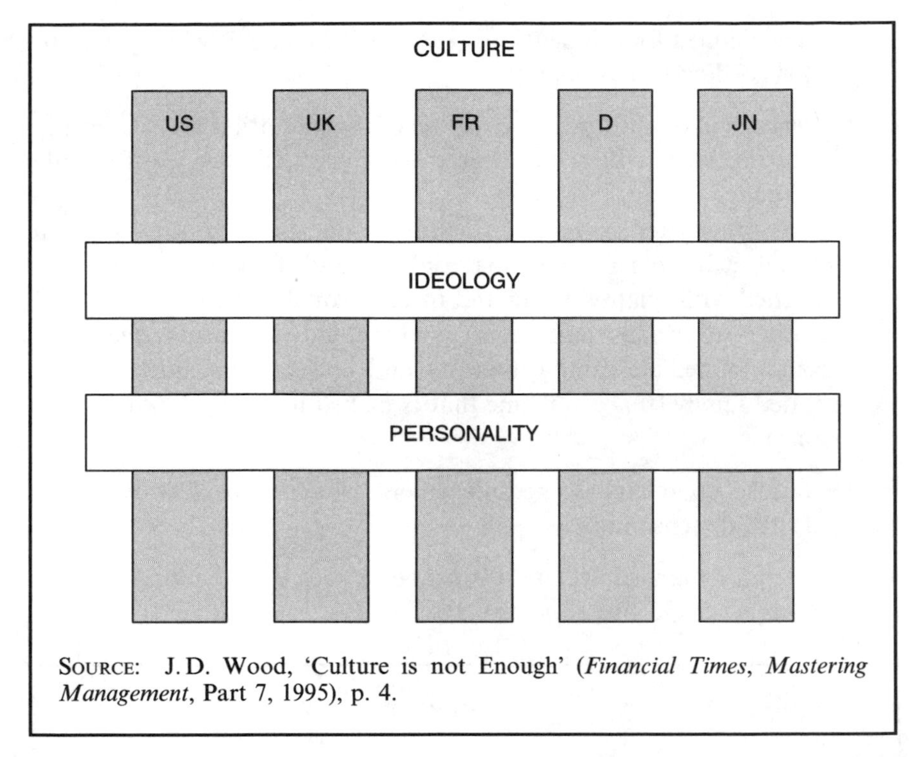

SOURCE: J. D. Wood, 'Culture is not Enough' (*Financial Times*, *Mastering Management*, Part 7, 1995), p. 4.

Figure 9.1 A culture matrix: hypothesised relationship between culture, ideology and personality

UK, France, Germany and Japan. Wood's observations underlie the fact that behaviour is determined only in part by national characteristics; ideologies and personalities are also important in determining how people will act. Nonetheless, employees, buyers, suppliers and shareholders do express different culturally defined attributes which have implications for the corporate brand – especially when we are dealing with a service where the 'people element' is very significant.

Work by Geert Hofstede into the work-related attitudes and values of 72 000 IBM employees from 40 different countries demonstrated that the values held by employees are culturally determined.[9] This does not contradict Wood's assertions about culture as Hofstede's work only looks at the vertical national dimensions and does not seek to analyse personality or ideological segments across the organisation. If one did, there might be more congruence of attitude by function – an engineering approach to problems that ran across the organisation, irrespective of national culture.

Hofstede defined four dimensions (Figures 9.2 and 9.3) which could be mapped according to nationality:

- concentration of authority: the degree of centralisation and leadership
- structuring of activities: the degree to which activities are formally structured
- gender orientation: where masculine values are concerned with personal achievement and materialism and feminine values are concerned with quality of life and interpersonal relations
- individualism versus collectivism: where individualism equates to personal/immediate family interests and collectivism equates to an extended family (this is a theme that is picked up on by Fukuyama in *Trust*[10])

Hofstede also conducted some subsequent work in the Far East and added a fifth dimension:

- Confucian dynamism: refers to whether a society has a long-term or short-term perspective (Figure 9.4).

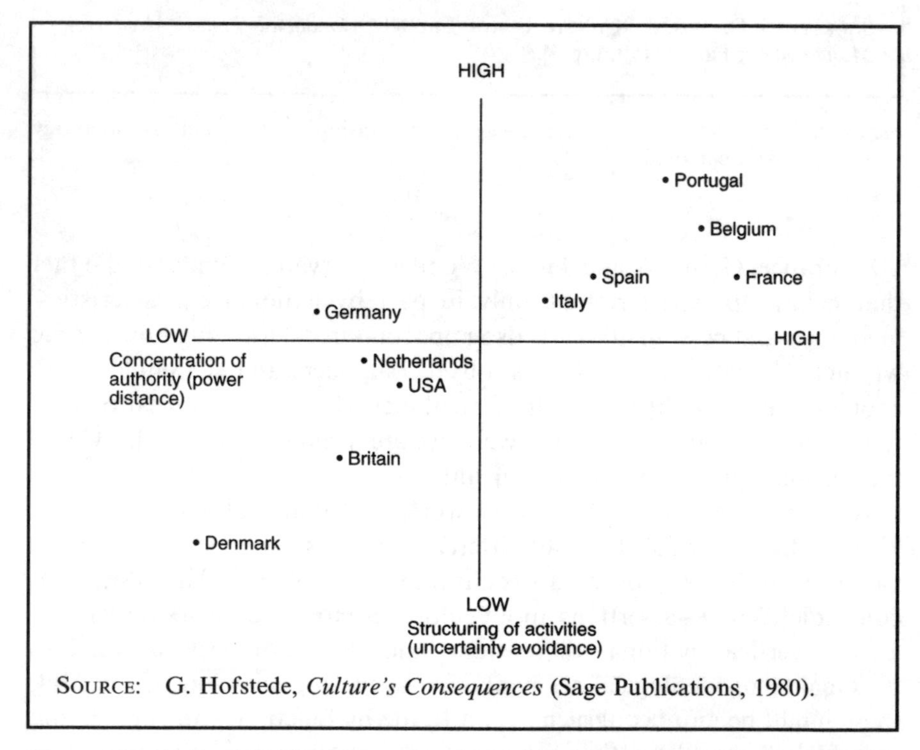

SOURCE: G. Hofstede, *Culture's Consequences* (Sage Publications, 1980).

Figure 9.2 Hofstede's dimensions of national culture: concentration of power and structuring of activities, selected European countries and USA, 1980

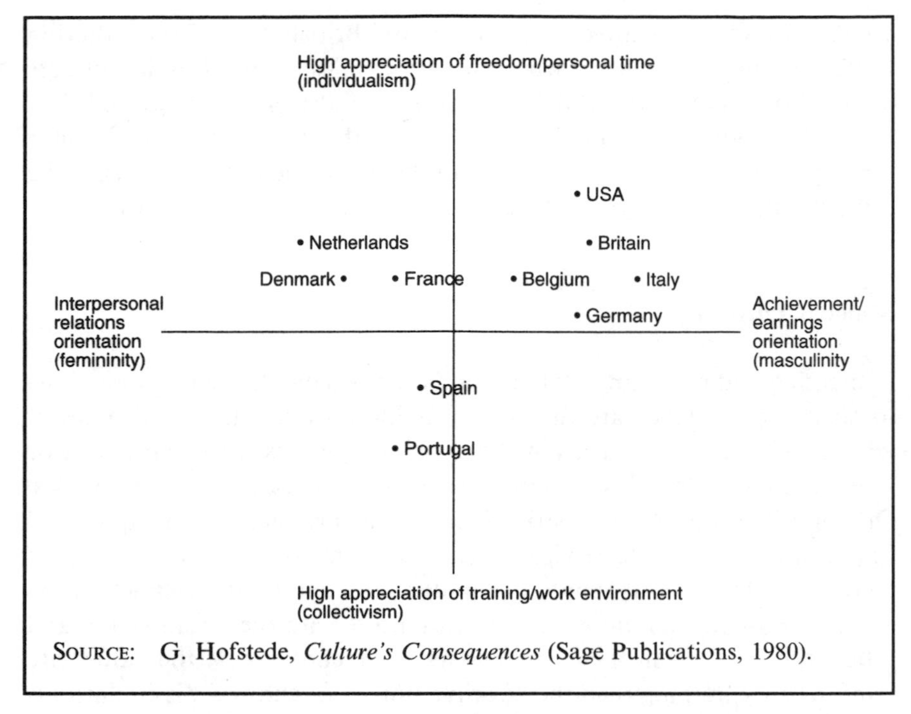

SOURCE: G. Hofstede, *Culture's Consequences* (Sage Publications, 1980).

Figure 9.3 Hofstede's dimensions of national culture: freedom, interpersonal relations, achievement/earnings and appreciation of work environment, selected European countries and USA, 1980

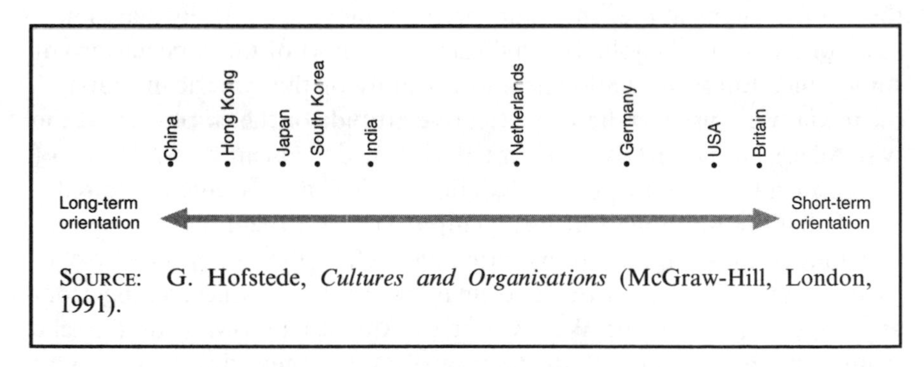

SOURCE: G. Hofstede, *Cultures and Organisations* (McGraw-Hill, London, 1991).

Figure 9.4 Confucian dynamism, Europe and USA

What can be observed from Figures 9.2–9.4 is perhaps what we feel intuitively: that in the USA and UK people have short-term orientations whereas Chinese and Japanese people are willing to take a long-term perspective; that French managers are autocratic and Danish ones somewhat relaxed; that German and Southern European organisations are very structured relative to American and British ones. These differing values are only too evident when two companies from different cultures merge. For example the BMW acquisition of Rover demonstrated very aptly the highly structured approach of the German manufacturer relative to the more short-termist and relaxed attitude of the British. The difficulty that global brands face is in managing this cultural diversity.

Managing diversity

In creating and managing global brands the real challenge is people: how to achieve consistency around core principles, while allowing degrees of adaptation to meet the needs of stakeholder segments either nationally or internationally? The first point to note is the issue of core principles. Organisations that have clearly defined and articulated principles will find it easier to replicate service levels in different countries. Employees of Johnson & Johnson or Apple Computer are buying into distinct values and are consequently more likely to empathise with the organisation and reflect those values in their dealings with stakeholders. If the values are reinforced by training then the negative impact of cultural dissimilarity is likely to be minimised. However, unless management is sensitive, cultural expectations can still get in the way. Disneyland in Paris faced initial problems with the quality of service provided by its employees, because the staff brought a French – and perhaps more specifically Parisian – sense of service to the job. This fell some way short of the expectations of some other European nationals and certainly of the American management who were used to the very attentive attitude of the employees at the two American-based Disney theme parks. The problem was not one of core principles, – Disney has well defined beliefs and is much admired – but the failure to imbue European employees with them.

Although most organisations' principles reflect their country of origin to some degree – it is difficult to imagine Apple or Nike coming from anywhere other than the West Coast of America or BMW or Porsche from anywhere other than Germany – as they develop, global organisations are likely to become less culturally defined. The increasing prevalence of non-nationals on the Boards of global companies, job rotation, international communication procedures and organisational learning in the context of different cultures can all help to evolve the corporate brand in increasingly non-national ways. In this way affinity with a specific national culture becomes less important while affinity with the organisational culture becomes more so. In Wood's terminology, employees are partly motivated to join an organisation because of the transnational ideology and personality.[11] Schein also notes that organizational cultures are a mix of national and corporate cultures:

> At the organizational level, the core assumption about the nature of human nature – that is, how workers and managers are viewed – will, no doubt, reflect the more basic assumptions of the host culture, but each organization will also build up its own elaborations of such assumptions.[12]

However, many organisations are still on the path to becoming global brands. Many are merely multinational: organisations that think internationally and set strategy accordingly. They may be structured along global product lines rather than by region or nationality, but they probably still retain a strong sense of national heritage at the centre – where all key decisions are made – and national cultures in their outposts. The indigenous culture rather than a corporate culture is dominant. This is exemplified by the lack of international expertise on the boards of supposedly global companies. In spite of the rationale for non-national Board directors, a 1989 Conference Board study concluded that:

> It would not appear that adding non-US citizen board members is a high priority for most US companies. Just 5 percent of the manufacturing companies and 2 percent in both the financial and nonfinancial service industry categories are considering it.[13]

This is supported by research undertaken by Winfried Ruigrok:

> Winfried Ruigrok, a visiting researcher at Warwick Business School, investigated the degree to which the world's top 100 companies (as defined by the Fortune Global 500) have actually internationalised. Result? While sales have become more international, the location of production and the appointment of board members is still dominated by national links.[14]

For these semi-global companies, change requires a recognition that there is a different way of doing things. It necessitates a company understanding the cultures of the regions in which it operates and listening to the needs of its stakeholders – whether they be consumers or employees. For example, New Holland, the international agricultural and earth-moving manufacturer employs some 19 000 people throughout the world. Its structure is based not on nationality, but on global product lines, it invests heavily in training and communication and has a multinational management team. Where relevant the product is adapted to the needs of the local market – such that it sells small tractors in Southern Europe where landholdings are often small and large machinery in the USA and Canada. Externally the company is a consistent communicator, with rigorous application of its visual identity and strong advertising. Yet in spite of all this work the company still had a series of distinct and competing national cultures. Partly this was a result of the nature of the organisation's growth through alliances and mergers, the most notable of which was the coming together of Fiat Agri and New Holland. To help generate a consistent corporate image the company recognised that it had to listen to its employees to try and develop a global organisational culture that drew on the positive aspects of the various parts of the company. The future task for the company will be to reinforce the positive aspects through improved cultural understanding and employee communications. The task is to gear the cultural evolution so that it is supportive of the organisational strategy. This approach recognises that absolute uniformity – especially of those corporate brand defining, employees – is utopian and may be undesirable. In fact a level of cultural diversity should be seen as a positive factor in helping organisations grow and learn:

> cultural diversity is a fact of cross-border life and it is the responsibility of the international manager to harness the opportunity it offers.[15]

A global image

Having accepted that the cultural affinities of individual employees means some degree of variability in the corporate brand delivery, what are the specific issues relating to global marketing communications ? Is it possible to co-ordinate the delivery of marketing communications so that the corporate brand has a consistent world-wide presentation? Following, the creation of Unisys, the visual identity, advertising, and literature were all strictly controlled by the head office in Philadelphia. The principle behind this approach was to signal the cohesion and control of the new company, and to try and create quickly a clear idea of what the new organisation stood for. Over time, the reins were loosened to allow operating companies in different countries a degree of adaptation. The campaign was successful both in terms of awareness and recall. Similarly, when Apple launched its Powerbook laptop computer range in Europe, it decided to develop an international campaign to run in 16 countries. Given the autonomy normally enjoyed by national operations and their agencies, this was difficult to manage. However, a campaign was developed conceptually in France and then implemented locally. This resulted in a fair uniformity of tone and message but did lead to some variability in the execution. These two examples demonstrate the positives and negatives of trying to achieve consistent presentations:

- Consistency is possible only when there is a single and sufficiently powerful source of authority. In the case of Unisys, the whole campaign in all media was controlled by the international corporate communications director.
- Implementation has to take account of the organisational structure. If countries traditionally enjoy significant autonomy then trying to impose campaigns from the centre will be hard fought.
- In organisations with diversified authority, maintaining tight central control is not a long-term option.

Thus, absolute consistency even in marketing communications is hard to achieve. The task for the international corporate communications manager is to define the essence of the corporate brand and those aspects which need to be tightly controlled and those which can be locally adapted. Generally the consistent points should be formed by those attributes which help identify a company to its stakeholders and reflect its overall personality. To continue with the example of Apple Computer, the points of consistency are the company name and logo, the typeface used, a clean, user-friendly approach to hardware and software design and an empowering theme to communications, developed from the early 1980s' advertising line: 'of the 235 million people in America, only a fraction can use a computer. Introducing Macintosh. For the rest of us.' The surprising aspect of Apple's advertising is that in spite of locally-produced campaigns, which in normal circumstances are not internationally co-ordinated, there is a strong continuity of theme – which is at least in part defined by not being IBM. Compare, for example, the tone of the famous *1984* advertisement which was created by US agency Chiat/Day and directed by Ridley Scott. It showed a big brother character on a large screen berating grey faced automatons. In runs a girl with a large hammer, pursued by thought police, who throws the hammer at the big brother image destroying the screen and liberating the workers.

> The ad [*1984*] argues that computers will add another element of democratisation to society. Rather than having some big computer in a basement somewhere which only a few people would have access to, Apple's hope was to take that power and put it on the desk of every individual, giving everyone the same access to information.[16]

In France, some years later, Apple developed a campaign called *Heir*. This was another cultural statement advertisement in which an old-fashioned company is being presented by a father to his son, who one day will inherit it. The landscape is bleak and the father's view of management is autocratic:

> all these people who will be working for you are there to execute tasks and not to think. If they ever started to think, they would want to start changing things.

However the end voiceover tells us: 'there are various ways of running a business and this is one of them. Luckily there are others.' In neither *1984* nor *Heir* is there a computer in sight. Without trying to overtly co-ordinate consistent communications, Apple achieve a distinctive and uniform presentation of the corporate brand. The significant points of international variability in Apple's approach are not in this area of marketing communications, but more in such areas as dealer support and point of sale activity. Apple's approach is also reflected by other powerful international corporate brands such as Nike, who likewise retain tight control over the organisational visual identity but run advertising campaigns which are locally produced but consistent to the Nike 'Just do it' attitude.

The arguments for consistency are seemingly logical. Economies of communication can be achieved by producing international communication campaigns which can be run anywhere in the world with minor adaptation. This saves money on the production of material and helps ensure the corporate brand has a consistent voice – especially important with the ever-increasing mobility of consumers. Wouldn't it be confusing if Sony had a different name or logo in different countries? Probably it would. As we travel abroad we see Sony on products in shops and in advertising; we buy Sony products in duty-free outlets; and we see Sony neon signs. By and large names and logos should be seen as an upstream issue and tightly controlled from the centre or by the relevant business unit in the case of a subsidiary. But the more we move downstream the more the arguments for adaptability strengthen. It is a false economy of communication if literature or advertising is slavishly replicated around the world yet is damaging to a local business. If a company is trying to market itself in a country where it has high awareness, it can probably concentrate on communicating the attributes that make it different. However, when the company enters a new market, where perhaps it has no awareness, it may find it has to establish simply what it does, before it can move on to other messages. The communication objectives, and consequently the executions, need to be different to be effective. As noted already, communications should be about building a relationship with stakeholders, and a company rarely has the same relationship with all its stakeholders. Some evidence for the variability of awareness across different cultures was provided by design consultants, Landor whose research among 9000 consumers showed that very few brands have uniform esteem – the 'study suggests that few brands have yet achieved true global status'.[17] The top 10 brands for different regions are listed in Table 9.1.

Similarly the regularly run surveys by *Management Today* in the UK and *Fortune* in the USA, into the most admired companies among business executives reveals considerable parochialism. The top two for 1996 in the UK were Tesco and Marks and Spencer, neither of which is well known in the USA – not least because historically they have been UK-oriented retailers. In the USA companies such as Rubbermaid and Home Depot are rated, but in the UK there would be very little recognition of these corporate brands.

Table 9.1 Top 10 brands in various regions

USA	*Europe*	*Japan*
Coca-Cola	Coca-Cola	Sony
Campbell	Sony	National
Disney	Mercedes	Mercedes
Pepsi-Cola	BMW	Toyota
Kodak	Philips	Takashimaya
NBC	Volkswagen	Rolls Royce
Black and Decker	Adidas	Seiko
Kellogg	Kodak	Matsushita
McDonald's	Nivea	Hitachi
Hershey	Porsche	Suntory

SOURCE: P. Kotler and G. Armstrong, *Marketing – An Introduction*, 3rd edn (Prentice-Hall, 1993).

Building a global corporate brand

As this chapter has noted, being a successful global brand is full of contradictions. While economies of production and communication encourage consistency the need to be competitive in local markets encourages adaptation. Neil Vander Dussen, vice chairman of Sony of America says:

> We must be more global, more localized, more integrated and more decentralized. These four characteristics may seem contradictory. But they are in fact mutually supportive.[18]

Building a global brand requires the management of these contradictions. Being more 'global' means earning trust with all of an organisation's stakeholders throughout the world by consistent quality and service and consistent values and branding. We have already looked at some of the difficulties in maintaining consistent quality and service, especially when a company lacks control over more downstream activities. However, most organisations could and should be able to build a consistent approach to branding. The first and most obvious element of global corporate branding is a consistent approach to naming. The truly global corporate brands employ the same name everywhere: Nike, Apple, Microsoft, Sony, McDonald's and IBM. This ubiquity is made easier by the largely organic growth of most of these brands. Companies that have grown through acquisition or joint ventures face a harder task. The FTSE 100 company De La Rue, the world's leading printer of bank notes had a phase until the early 1990s when it was highly acquisitive. The company acquired companies in bank security, lottery systems, counting machines and security print. Along with the acquisitions came a plethora of corporate brand names: Faraday and LeFebure in the USA, Garny in Germany, ILS in the Netherlands and Lerchundi in Spain. Even in the UK, the company had two corporate brands: Thomas De La Rue and De La Rue. In its desire to build a global brand, the company recognised it ideally needed to have one name throughout the world. However, the barrier the company faced was that De La Rue had little or no awareness in either Germany or the USA. Should the company discard long-established corporate brands, such as LeFebure and Garny. In the end the move was undertaken gradually with most local corporate brands being given the prefix 'De La Rue' and tied in to a global corporate style through a visual identity programme.

In determining name choices, the longer-term needs of global uniformity need to be considered alongside the short-term requirement to manage on-going business. Whatever the resolution, it is almost always better to retain or adapt existing names, rather than create new corporate brands, which will inevitably take a long time to establish. In building a global brand, when an organisation enters a new market it needs to earn the trust of its stakeholders. Government and legislators need to be convinced of the company's probity and commitment – especially if the company is making an acquisition in a new country. Government, such as in the case of BAT's acquisition of the US insurance company, Farmers, can be obstructive to an organisation if it considers a company not to be acting in the national or local interest. Alternatively government can welcome companies such as Nissan or Sony for their inward investment. Similarly global brands need to have the support of local communities, unions and employees, especially if they are significant local employers, such as BP America in Cleveland in the USA or Nissan at Sunderland in the UK. Also, ideally, consumers need to have a positive attitude towards a brand. All of this requires trust, which can be earned only by performance over time. However, the corporate brand starts with an advantage if it already has a strong global brand and reputation to go with it. It then brings a track record that at least professional audiences, such as potential investors and the media, can take into account. The danger that the corporate brand must guard against is arrogance: that because an organisation has a strong reputation in several countries, it will find awareness and favour in a new one.

On some occasions, corporate brand names do not work internationally. The name itself might be difficult to pronounce – although Daewoo and Hyundai show that perhaps as we become more cosmopolitan this barrier is reducing. Or it might become limiting because it no longer accurately describes a business: USX (once US Steel) changed its name because of its interest in oil production. Or the geography might carry too many connotations. First National City Bank of New York found it easier to market itself internationally as Citibank, Federal Express has rebranded itself as FedEx and British Telecom has become BT. However we do still have Royal Dutch Shell, American Express and Deutsche Bank. The route to analysing corporate brand naming is through research. If the strategy is to be a global brand and the national heritage is misunderstood or is negative, then it may be worth considering dropping or amending an overtly national name. However, if the national heritage is an asset – as many airlines perceive it to be – then the name should probably be left alone. Given the trauma (and expense) of a name change, the arguments for it need to be powerful.

Global visual identities

Visual consistency should be easier to achieve than verbal consistency – there is probably more emotion about what a company is called than how it is presented. However, the reality is that visual consistency for most global brands is hard won. In large organisations with decentralised decision making and authority over marketing decisions, there will be considerable temptation to tinker with the look of the global brand. Unless someone proselytises about the benefits of uniform branding, there is a tendency to see consistent use of typefaces, colours and logos as rather unimportant. The same arguments apply here as with brand naming. Audiences will be confused if the look of an organisation is distinctively different in Germany to that in Italy. People will ask is it the same corporate brand and is there a reason for the difference? Perhaps the company has different owners or sells different products? Maybe the quality of service will be different? If the look is consistent. then audiences will assume it is the same corporate brand with the same standards. The question then is: how can consistency be achieved?

When companies move from national to international to global brands, they normally take a visual style with them. Visual identities for companies such as Texaco, Shell, Rolls-Royce and Coca-Cola have remained essentially unchanged throughout the twentieth century. The transition from national to global has not necessitated a radical reappraisal of their look. Generally a national identity will work in international markets; the exceptions, as with brand naming, are when the visual identity is in some way limiting to the company objectives. Corporate brands that want to appear as insiders and above nationality may find life difficult if they feature something overtly nationalistic in their visual identities – such as a flag or a national symbol. Alternatively a company may want to signal to its audiences its move to a global focus. For example, the Dutch chemicals company, Akzo, was seen to be nationally-oriented in spite of employing 70 000 people in 50 countries. As part of the process of signalling its global intentions, it revamped its visual identity to produce a symbol that was not culturally specific.

Occasionally there are arguments that a visual identity has colours or a symbol that is inappropriate in certain markets, but these instances are rare. It is certainly true that different cultures have differing ideas about these issues. In some countries, orange may be the fashionable colour, whereas in others green may carry greater weight. Although, some generalisations can be made about colour perceptions, such as that most countries associate blue with professionalism, trying to follow fashion trends in visual identity design is a dangerous pastime. Most identities have long lives – trying to use colours that work here and now may look very dated next year. The same is true of design styles. This doesn't argue against trying to create a contemporary feel to a design, but use of in-vogue typefaces or design signatures may in the longer term be inappropriate. Some of the most successful designs – perhaps with occasional facelifts – seem unerringly modern: BMW, Nike, Apple and Sony. In making, these judgements, the difficulty is of course divorcing the product from the visual identity. A better measure would be: are the visual identities appropriate to the corporate brand: do they suggest the sort of company and products that we would expect from their appearance? In the case of these four global brands, the answer is probably 'yes', although it could be argued that because we know the brands so well the tone of the visual identity is irrelevant. For companies entering new markets with perhaps a limited or non-existent reputation, the visual identity – the combination of type, colour and graphics – will be a key signal of what to expect from the corporate brand.

The task for the global corporate brand is to ensure that it has a system of visual signals that will help create an image that is appropriate and effective, and then to manage the signals so that they are consistently applied everywhere in the world. Whereas brand names within the corporate portfolio may vary, there is little argument for the long-term retention of several visual identities by the corporate brand. Even in the previously cited De La Rue example, when the American and German brands retained their names they still used the De La Rue global logotype as a signifier of their inclusion in the group. The task for management, then, is to ensure effective implementation of the visual identity, so that there is a consistent tone to all communications no matter from which part of the world they emanate. This requires management to demonstrate through words and actions that the visual identity does matter, and to institute briefing and design systems to ensure that globally recognised and adhered-to guidelines are in place.

Adaptable elements

While naming and visual identity should by and large be consistent elements of the global brand, elements such as advertising, direct marketing and public relations may need to be more adaptable. Building relationships with consumers and other audiences is difficult to achieve through a standardised approach. Direct marketing, in particular, while being in tune perhaps with a global tone, needs to be adapted to the vagaries of local markets. Yet, in the desire to achieve global economies of communication, some corporate brands ignore the value of adaptation. This may be valid if international segments with similar attitudes can be targeted effectively. Companies such as British Airways and Coca-Cola have proved that communications can be consistent in many markets, but there are probably many more brands where the desire for consistency leads to either bland executions which will work in any market or less than effective communications. As a measure of the inappropriateness of many campaigns one has only to look at TV comedy shows built around the showing of other countries advertising campaigns which draw on different cultural precedents. An example from personal experience was the campaign developed in the USA for a mid-market fragrance. The tone of the campaign itself was overly romanticised and researched poorly in European markets. The name of the brand, which was called after a famous American designer, achieved high awareness in the USA and communicated connotations of wealth and sophistication. In Europe, the designer name was virtually unknown and carried little in the way of cachet. However, the desire for a global approach led to the same branding, advertising and point-of-sale approach as in the USA. The brand's life was average and short-lived.

Advertising for Nescafé, Absolut Vodka, Nike and Apple all started out as national campaigns, but became global (sometimes with relevant adaptation) in other markets, because of their success at home. This approach often seems to be just as effective (if not more so) than campaigns that are devised to be international from the outset. The campaign for Nescafé's Gold Blend, for example, started out as a purely national affair, but ended up being adapted for the USA and Latin America. Built around the on-going soap story of Gold Blend as a catalyst for two people to meet and then form a relationship, the advertising was so successful that the company decided to run the campaign in the USA, although it had to be amended because the brand had a different name. Similarly, the cool, understated sexual attraction between the couple seemed to work well in Anglo-Saxon markets, but in Latin America something more overtly sexual was needed. The soap opera theme was retained, but the film was reshot with lascivious looks, full of innuendo. To British and American eyes the Latin American campaign is funny rather than sensual.

When dealing with more specific audiences, such as suppliers and buyers, government and the media, global approaches are likely to have even less validity. Although the tone of communications should be maintained to avoid contradictions, the needs of most of these audiences are country-specific. American newspapers are generally not very interested in the business thinking of a London-based company, unless it has a relevant impact on America. The media relations activity of an organisation therefore needs to be rooted in national markets, so that the 'local' angle can be stressed. This applies equally to government audiences. It is nigh-on impossible to build a relationship with government representatives if one is geographically distant from them. Relationships of this type – as with a company's buyers and suppliers – need proximity to be effective. The task for the organisation, as the Sony quote on p. 150 so effectively put it, is to be more global and more localized. Communications strategy at the global level needs to have a global orientation – a consistent positioning and tone needs to be developed and disseminated. Those elements that define the global corporate brand need to be sacrosanct. Product adaptation and communications implementation can vary as the needs of the local market dictates.

Summary

True global brands – of which there are very few – plan and manage on a global basis. They transcend nationality both in their thinking and their cultures. The dominant element in their make-up is not national heritage – although there may be some elements of this – but a global corporate culture. To create a global corporate brand requires the integration of a consistent approach to human resources, so that service levels and employee attitudes and behaviour are similar in all countries – a measure of the strength of the corporate brand – together with a consistency in the tone of marketing communications. The latter should be easier to achieve, but companies need to understand which elements of the communication system benefit from being consistent and which work best through local adaptation. There will always be people who are in favour of adapting everything, but local managers need to be made aware as to which elements of the corporate brand are inviolable. The task of getting this right requires effective analysis and management. Generally the more downstream an activity, the greater the requirement for localisation.

10 Managing the Corporate Brand

One of the core themes of this book has been the need for the corporation to manage the often conflicting and interactive relationships with its various audiences. The differing perspectives of customers, shareholders, employees, local communities and the media all need to be understood; the organisation needs to develop plans to meet the requirements of these audiences, and someone has to make the plans work. This requires an integrated approach: needs cannot be balanced if the focus is on only one group or audience. Simply serving the needs of shareholders, which might come under the responsibility of the Group Financial Officer, may impact negatively on the relationship with customers and employees. Yet the reality in most organisations is that relationships are narrowly defined. Marketing Directors' experience and remit tends to be focused on managing relationships with consumers. They tend not to be experts in shareholder or employee communications, which is far more likely to come under the Financial Department and Human Resources, respectively. Relationships with specific audiences, such as the media and government, will often be allocated to Corporate Affairs. Unless, there is a figure with over-arching responsibility for all communications – a rarity – the only figure with enough weight to integrate the process is the Chief Executive. The CEO is in many ways ideal for this role – strategy should be a combination of operations and communication – but CEOs too often place singular emphasis on the operative aspects at the expense of communications. From experience, there have been only one or two CEOs who believed in and controlled strategic communications such that continuity of tone was achieved in all messages. In most cases, though the CEO might argue that corporate image or communications is vital to the success of the business, it will still tend to be seen as an after-thought.

To raise the stakes in the battle for recognition, Charles Fombrun suggests that organisations should create a new executive role: the chief reputation officer (CRO),

> The CRO's tactical responsibilities would include oversight of pricing, advertising, quality, environmental compliance, investor relations,

public affairs, corporate contributions and employee, customer and media relations. Rather than literally do each of these jobs the CRO would act as a corporate guide, working with specialists in each area to help them see the reputation consequences of their decisions.[1]

The ideal of a CRO is laudable, but it is hard to envisage this as a separate individual, competing for influence with Corporate Affairs and Marketing. A more achievable aim would be to encourage marketing personnel to broaden their roles so that their remit includes the co-ordination of communication with all audiences. The barrier here is the nature of much marketing education, which focuses on consumers (and occasionally professional buyers) to the exclusion of other audiences. If marketing students learn about the existence of other audiences it tends to be on corporate identity or communication electives. In the short term it is difficult therefore to see a change in the skills of marketers. The most observably effective route to integration is that adopted by companies such as BT, and some departments of government, who through cross-functional teams are working on achieving a community of purpose across the organisation. The BT approach uses groups of specialists working together to question briefs and to adopt a broad perspective to communications.

> Within BT there are three main customer facing divisions: personal communications, business communications and global communications. Each is vertically integrated . . . we also have a brand and reputation team, which is a fourth arm. It's responsible for the management and maintenance of the brand, the brand expression and corporate identity system. So it's a cross divisional function.'[2]

In this system people meet informally all the time but additionally there are regular meetings at which all departments are represented. To be successful it needs a sympathetic culture and the willingness of people to work together. Its big advantage is that rather than trying to make specialists into something they are not, it pools specialisms to achieve breadth of understanding and consistency of message. Can this idea of putting communication specialists together in integrated teams work anywhere? As long as the teams are listened to rather than just being a discussion shop, and the organisational barriers do not actively discourage horizontal communications, then the answer should be yes. It simply requires the organisation to recognise the inter-relatedness of audiences and communications.

Communications and operations

Vital to the effective management of integrated communications is the close relationship between communications and operations. The danger in an all-powerful communications function is that it becomes removed – sometimes physically to a strategic headquarters – from the day-to-day manufacture of a product or offering of a service. This has the potential to lead to communications out of touch with organisational reality. In planning and executing communications there needs to be a close co-ordination with the means of production. Communication needs to reflect both the nature and personality of the product – it can do this only if communicators understand its attributes. They need to understand how a product is made, what employees feel about a product and how consumers might use it. This should not encourage people to take an inward, production-led view of what they market, but it should provide a depth that sometimes seems to be missing from marketing communications. In a benchmarking study looking at how 'excellent' design management organisations achieve quality of output, one of the constant themes was the close relationship of design briefs to key business objectives. All the organisations adhered to the belief that design was not some aesthetic tool but an integral part of communicating the essence of the organisation. This in turn led to considerable emphasis being placed on the development of the brief itself and much training time was devoted to getting this aspect of the process right.[3] The key benefit of ensuring that marketing communications are an accurate reflection of organisational reality is that communications as a totality – the combination of communications and operations – is both credible and consistent.

Managing consistency

Consistency is an ideal. In most diversified organisations, persuading those responsible for communications to adhere to basic rules concerning message or colour or type is difficult enough, but trying to integrate the thoughts and actions of individuals makes it nearly impossible. The reality is achieving partial rather than absolute consistency. The question then is: how can this be achieved? As suggested earlier it can't be imposed – although guidelines may help. The simplest and most effective way is if people believe not in the rules defining how they should act, but in the principles that formed them. In organisations with clearly communicated principles the achievement of this aim will be easier than in an organisation where the principles are vague. Core principles not only help to ensure that people start from similar points, it helps to provide everyone with an almost intuitive feeling for the right course of action in any given situation. Consistency may not be absolute, but it is far more likely. An interesting example of an organisation that is struggling to achieve this continuity is The Church of England. Its difficulty as an organisation reflects that confronted by many diversified organisations with devolved decision making. The Church is headed by the Archbishop of Canterbury and the Archbishop of York and 44 bishops who control areas known as dioceses. Within the dioceses there are some 11 000 priests who run local churches. The Church has its own parliament – the Synod – its own committees and a communication department. The operational and communication problem it faces is the nature of the relationship between the component parts of the organisation. It is not a command and control structure as in the Catholic church. The centre can only advise – 'shepherd' – the bishops and the priests, but should a bishop want to contradict or pursue a course different to other bishops, there is very little anyone can do to restrain him. Although there are some beliefs that unite most clerics, there is nonetheless a broad range of thought within the Church. Whenever there is a crisis issue, such as homosexuality, the Church cannot act with one voice, whatever anyone recommends. The ensuing image, fostered by the media who receive different views as well, is one of chaos.

The nature of the relationship between the centre and the component parts is aptly demonstrated through the nature of communications. The centre itself, formed from a variety of standing committees, produces communications material which is varied in its tone and content. The dioceses, with their long historical traditions, often eschew such items as the cruciform in favour of the Bishop's coat of arms and the words the 'Diocese of' rather than any mention of the Church of England. The parishes, who enjoy considerable autonomy, again create their own communications standards without any reference to any other further authority. The collective result is one where the key Christian symbol – the Cross – is largely unused and the organisational name is lost within 'divisional' brands. To draw a commercial analogy, it is as if McDonalds decided to stop using its 'm' device and changed its name each time to the location from which it operated. How should the Church extricate itself from this problem? Ideally, it requires a fundamental change of structure and a change in the nature of the contract between the elements of the organisational hierarchy. In the absence of this, the best it can achieve is a very partial and gradual move towards greater consistency. To help effect this transformation, the Church has embarked on a programme of trying to improve the flow of information from the centre. Two initiatives have been implemented:

- Make sure people are informed about the viewpoint of the centre. While the centre cannot impose its views on dioceses or anyone else, it can ensure through faxes, memos, newsletters and e-mail that the relevant people are quickly informed as to the Church's desired stand on any particular issue. This will not lead to slavish adherence to the 'party line', but it does create the opportunity for continuity.
- Set an example at the centre by creating consistent and relevant communications. All printed communications can and should be created around common standards by using a consistent approach to branding (the Cross), typography, colour and message. If the centre can get the tone right and provide effective communications to its members, then it is more likely to be able to persuade others as to the relevance of the approach.

Once the centre gets it communications working effectively, it needs to provide the resources to help persuade the dioceses to integrate their communications. Partly this will be achieved through training of the individuals responsible within the dioceses and partly it will be achieved by creating a set of guidelines that people can use to steer their approach to communications. No one envisages that this will be a rapid or complete process, but over time the aim is to achieve greater consistency by setting an example and helping support others. In a commercial organisation, the situation described above is expedited by the ability of the organisation to impose its will more readily, and perhaps a greater cohesion – the Church of England encompasses a very broad collection of passionately held views. However there are still strong points of similarity. Heads of business units can be equally obstructive in their desire to retain their own distinctive style of communications even in the face of hostility from the centre. And achieving continuity is still best achieved through a programme of persuasion and recognised benefits rather than some rigid system. Involvement is preferable to imposition.

To build consensus, it is best to involve employees in any communication process. Employee suggestions should be sought, the results of employee research should be fed back into the organisation and cross-functional teams should be allowed their input. In addition the following mechanisms can be used to aid understanding and stimulate involvement:

- presentations and seminars to explain the nature of consistent communications and its benefits
- the development of groups to work on broadly-based communication issues and to discuss best practice
- the creation of a steering group, involving people from different divisions and functions, to help create organisational communication standards
- training and development focusing on key communication issues
- regular reviews to assess the quality of communications.

Using benchmarks

Although the Church of England is a rather idiosyncratic organisation there are some lessons that can be learned from it. Not least of these is that there are no universal approaches to corporate branding. A corporate brand is a unique entity and therefore its management needs to take account of the specific structure and culture of the organisation. A company that believes in openness and the multi-directional flow of communication among autonomous business units will need a different approach to an organisation that is centralised and cautious about the way it disseminates information. Although we might generally believe that empowerment is a good thing, some people would prefer not to be empowered and some organisations will claim that when they have tried to empower people it hasn't worked. The reasons for this might be various, including that empowerment is not something you simply proclaim – rather it needs to be nurtured within a sympathetic culture. Whatever the rationale, the corporate experience will simply refute the principle. However, while accepting the need for an adaptive approach to the management of the corporate brand, qualitative benchmarking – supported by the evidence of quantitative benchmarks which evaluate the effectiveness of communication spend – suggests there are some common elements of good communicators.

Be good listeners

> The Japanese explain their ideal concept of a company as one giant feedback loop which continually joins up the identification of consumer needs and the satisfying of them.[4]

Organisations that manage communications well, listen well – and not only to consumers. They listen to the ideas of their employees, they take note of what their shareholders say and they build relationships with media and other influential audiences. They adhere to the notion that communication is an interactive process. Relevant communications are not achieved by imagining what people need to know, it is about understanding what they need. This does not abrogate the need for management to make decisions – research cannot determine the best way of doing something – but it can inform decision making and can sometimes stimulate truly different ways of doing things. Of course, some people argue that listening to consumers will only ever deliver variations of what exists already. Take the view of Chrysler:

> Being customer-driven is certainly a good thing, but if you're so customer-driven that you're merely following yesterday's trends, then, ultimately, customers won't be driving your supposedly customer-driven products.[5]

Similarly, Sony claim that no amount of research could have told them about the Walkman. Its creation was a combination of lateral thinking and intuition. There are many other examples of intuitive new product development but equally there are other seemingly good ideas which fail to find a market. Although many inventors and designers see research as the enemy of innovation in reality it should be seen as part of its stimulus.

Rely on experts

Some organisations do maintain in-house design groups or artwork teams or copywriters, but large organisations increasingly prefer to outsource these activities and use internal resources to set up strategies. Many large companies now have groups of communication professionals who act as internal consultants to communication commissioners within the organisation. Their role is more to do with enabling others to produce effective communications rather than doing. The argument for going external is that communication buyers can have the pick of specialist skills rather than being constrained by what they have internally. Some companies build up rosters of approved external agencies, while others rely on the judgement of advisors as to who should undertake a specific job. In all cases, the companies expect to build close and open relationships with their suppliers. They try to overcome professional jealousy and non-cooperation by a clearly visible and even-handed approach to the commissioning of work. Suppliers recognise how their expertise is viewed and are discouraged from encroaching on each other.

Develop a rigorous approach to briefing

All the good communicators place great emphasis on briefing systems and making sure that briefs are as tight and as accurate as possible. This has several benefits. First, arguing through the brief often helps to really define what the organisation is trying to achieve. It thus sets up a questioning process that ensures the motivation for the brief is rational. Second, the time spent on getting the brief right encourages people to question the business objectives behind it. Third, it sets out the points of accountability in any given project. Fourth, it helps the consultancy to focus on the real issues. Some organisations have a set way of creating briefs, while for others the approach is looser, but there is always intellectual rigour in the process.

Believe in training

In most large organisations, there are many people who hold funds for marketing activity. With the emergence of desk top publishing (DTP) programmes there are also many people who believe they can best communicate their idea of the corporate brand through their own creative efforts. The only way to counter the visual and verbal chaos that ensues is through training. Communication commissioning employees need to be trained in the art of briefing, in the use of external consultancies and in how to judge work. All excellent companies invest heavily in the process of building up the skills of these people.

Have a supportive leadership

Without leaders who believe in the importance of communication, any programme will founder through either passive or active undermining. Active undermining is where senior managers endorse the principles of good communication, but then tell people it doesn't really matter. Passive undermining is where no obvious support is given to the communication programme. In both cases the signal to employees will be that communication is rather ephemeral. Although leaders of organisations will generally proclaim their belief in communication, the failure of senior managers to actively support it is the most common factor in poor communications. Again, the excellent companies either have a communications champion or champions, or they have developed cultures which place great emphasis on the importance of communications.

Never be satisfied

Excellent communicators never rest on their laurels. They monitor the effectiveness of their work, they conduct internal reviews and they question the way they do things. This doesn't mean continual change in tone and quality, it simply leads to a sharper focus.

The role of consultants

The corporate brand is an on-going entity. It does not suddenly appear, as if by magic, at the touch of a consultant's wand. An organisation will reveal itself all the time through the attitudes and actions of individuals, through the pronouncements of management, through the appearance of buildings and offices, through the nature of its products and services and through literature and newsletters. However, occasionally, an organisation needs to step back and question the way it does things. Sometimes it is hard for internal people to do this and consequently external consultants are called in. Of course, some consultants, such as a PR or advertising agency may be involved on a continuous basis, but others may well be called in to perform a specific task. The key to most client–consultant relationships is to recognise the transitory nature of the experience for the consultant. Any solution needs to work at the time it is implemented, but it needs to be owned by the organisation and its people, because the solution will need to be adaptive to changing circumstances. The organisation cannot realistically keep calling back the consultancy – although the consultant may like it – to solve everyday problems. This means that any recommendations have to take account of the organisation's capabilities. Even if the consultant stays to help manage the early phases of implementation, it is management that will have to make the recommendations work over time. Consultancy projects that produce well reasoned reports are all very well, but if the organisation cannot or will not implement the findings, it is an exercise in futility.

To try to overcome this problem the organisation needs to be careful in the selection of its consultants – ensuring that the consultancy has a good track record, is committed to effective implementation and is culturally compatible. Consultants should also only be called in once all key leaders are supportive of the initiative: rearguard action by recalcitrant directors will undermine any programme. Once the consultancy is in place they need to have access to all available information and to managers and employees. The collection of valid data can be through normal qualitative and quantitative means and/or through a more involved approach, such as action research, where the consultant participates in the organisational evolution. Whichever methodology is chosen, people need to know they can confide their views without fear of retribution and that comments will be treated confidentially. In most organisations people are only too happy to have the opportunity to tell an outsider what is wrong. The problem for the consultant in this context is judging the information received. However, in spite of the loquaciousness of most interviewees, there are occasions when the degree of mistrust in the organisation is such that co-operation from employees is very hard won. In these instances management need to communicate the rationale for the research and to stress the eventual benefits.

In the process of information collection, the consultant needs to be aware of likely stumbling blocks and potential resistance to recommendations. Spotted early, these areas can be handled. The best client–consultant relationships are based on teamwork – of consultancy and client working together to find solutions that will have longevity. This is the approach suggested by Chris Argyris in his *Intervention Theory and Method*[6] Argyris asserts there are three key requirements for intervening in an organisation:

- the consultant should help the client collect valid data about their problem
- the consultant should not prescribe or impose solutions, the authority of the client should be respected and the consultant should strive to help people make free, informed choices about their future actions
- the consultant should operate in a way that helps people to become internally committed to their chosen course of action. Therefore they will experience ownership of the change.This partnership approach is summarised in Argyris' organisational development model (Figure 10.1). This recognises that the consultant will find it difficult to effect organisational change without the authority of management and that the client as an insider will find it difficult to decipher the organisational assumptions and culture. In this method the consultant is not providing the answers so much as enabling the organisation to find its own solutions. The big advantage with this approach, if managed successfully is that the organisation can feel it owns the solution.

ACTION	CONVENTIONAL MODEL	ORGANIZATIONAL DEVELOPMENT MODEL
Problem definition	Client	Client ↔ Consultant
Data gathering	Consultant	Consultant ↔ Client
Data analysis	Consultant	Consultant ↔ Client
Problem diagnosis	Consultant	Client ↔ Consultant
Solution proposed	Consultant	Client ↔ Consultant
Action plan design	Consultant ↔ Client	Client ↔ Consultant
Implementation	Client	Consultant ↔ Client
Review	(Client)	Client ↔ Consultant

SOURCE: C. Argyris, *Intervention Theory and Method* (Addison-Wesley, 1970).

Figure 10.1 Intervention methods

The role of leaders

Effective communication is about signalling, consistently. Sometimes it is possible for organisations to signal their intent without the support of leaders. Some organisations are very effective at developing strong and consistent corporate brands through their marketing communications simply because they are good marketers. However the really sustainable corporate brands are those who get their internal communications right. As the writer and consultant, David Bernstein, observes: ‘the company that manages to communicate well internally, generally manages to communicate well externally. But the reverse is not necessarily the case.’ This is supported by Rosabeth Moss Kanter:

> Companies with strong communications across functions and widely shared information tend to have more productive external relationships.[7]

Effective internal communications can to some degree be effective without the active support of leadership, but it is far harder to achieve. Leaders are the people who show their commitment, or otherwise, to internal communications by their own actions and the value they place on informing employees about the organisation's direction and performance. It is the things they recognise and reward that will send signals to employees. And it is the congruity of their public pronouncements and private comments that signal consistency. Thus leadership is a vital element in both defining and sustaining the corporate brand by a commitment to sustaining the flow of vertical and horizontal communications. As Schein points out:

> Leaders do not have a choice about whether to communicate. They have a choice only about how much to manage what they communicate. Organizations differ in the degree to which the cultural messages are consistent and clear; and this variation in cultural clarity is probably a reflection of the clarity and consistency of the assumptions of the leaders.[8]

Summary

Managing the corporate brand is a high level activity and requires individuals who are able to coalesce operations and communications to create a consistent experience of the organisation. The problem that most organisations face in trying to achieve this is the split of communication roles among various people. However some companies get round this problem by forming cross-functional groups who adopt a broad perspective of the corporate brand. This approach seems well founded because it integrates the specialisms of individuals to form a synergistic whole. For most organisations, the reality is that communications can never be truly consistent, but the closer they come to consistency the better. Best practice in communications management suggests that this can be achieved by learning from other organisations that are committed to communications and who:

- are good listeners
- use consultants effectively
- develop a rigorous approach to briefing
- believe in training
- have the support of leaders
- are never satisfied.

11 Conclusion

The corporate brand is distinct from product brands in the diversity of audiences with which it has to interact. Rationally, it should not focus on shareholders to the detriment of others, nor just on consumers. The former leads to an obsession with profits to the exclusion of all else and the latter to an obsession with market share. Balancing the needs of audiences, then, should be the task of the complete corporate brand. Listening to and then meeting their requirements therefore makes good business sense. It makes the most of employees' abilities and initiative, it helps garner positive press comment, it generates the goodwill of shareholders and it meets the demands of consumers for good service. Citing the examples of Marks and Spencer, Unipart, John Lewis, Unilever and Shell, the writer John Plender says:

> These companies appear to be good at fostering what sociologists call social capital: the intangible wealth represented by education and training, cooperative working practices, loyalty and commitment. In businesses which rely heavily on human capital, stakeholding confers competitive advantage and, quite as important, encourages employees to feel good about what they do.[1]

As noted in Chapter 6, loyalty and commitment is a two-way relationship. It is conferred by employees in response to the way an employer acts. It is part of the source of unity that exists in many Japanese businesses where there is a mutual identification of needs, but is far rarer in Anglo–American business where the relationship is more contractually defined – and short-termist. Indeed the short-term concentration on profitability that is so evident in British and American businesses leads to an inherent fear among employees about their expendability. In the 1996 edition of *Social Trends*, research about views on trade unions is cited. It shows that whereas between 1989 and 1994 the proportion who thought that better pay was the top priority fell from 28% to 15%, the number who thought that to protect existing jobs was the priority rose from 28% to 37%.[2]

Is there an alternative to the stakeholder view? Although John Plender makes the distinction between companies who rely on human capital and those who do not, there are examples of organisations, such as the British electrical retailers, Dixons, who are dependent on human capital and do not adhere to the stakeholder view, and yet are very successful. Indeed many British and American businesses derive their source of competitive advantage from a seeming focus on profitability. However, with one or two exceptions, such as the conglomerate Hanson and leveraged buyout specialists, the profitability focus is a mirage. Dixons may not have an involving approach to its employee relations, but it is very strong at buying and merchandising which is the source of its competitive advantage. Other companies may make public pronouncements about their focus on enhancing shareholder value as a primary aim, but consumers and buyers do not purchase products and services to boost profitability. They buy because a product or a service meets a need. Shareholder value is a result of how well the organisation manages the fulfilment of that need. So although some companies may eschew the human capital approach we might pose the question: would their performance be further enhanced if they made full use of it?

The other counter-argument to the stakeholder view is that the two main exponents of it, Japan and Germany, are struggling to maintain their economic miracles. However this ignores the fact that the miracles would not have occurred without a balanced approach in the first place. Both countries have benefited from a unity of purpose between employers and employees and a strong focus on meeting consumer needs. The close relationship between banks and businesses has also allowed organisations to take a longer-term view of their strategies. The fact that both countries are suffering from an economic malaise is more to do with internal structural problems and the failure of the stakeholder system to adapt to the reality of the globalisation of finance. As is being discovered in all sorts of spheres, it is becoming increasingly difficult to inoculate any society against the ravages of globalisation. If Germany and Japan do adapt their systems to take account of these trends then the miracles will be back on track. The potential advantage for the free-wheeling Anglo–American model is that if it chooses the consensual way to balancing needs it should be able to marry the benefits of meeting the requirements of employees, local communities, government and customers with a more aggressive approach to finance. To achieve this will take a much improved understanding between companies and their financiers, and a willingness to look to the longer term.

The second element of the inclusive argument is that there is a general principle derived from research: that familiarity equals favourability (see Figure 1.1). Partly familiarity is concerned with the nature of a company's products; Ford is likely to be better known among a whole range of audiences because of the visibility of its products, compared with another *Fortune* 500 company, Bandag, who make truck tyre retreads. Partly it is to do with the relevance and consistency of messages emanating from the organisation. Once we recognise the inter-relatedness of many audiences – that consumers can also be shareholders and that journalists are also consumers – we should ensure that an organisation is communicating a consistent message to these individuals. Of course it is true that the journalist is in one mode when writing an article and in another when buying a product, but he or she is still the same individual.

Consistency operates by a simple premise. When an organisation has to compete for our attention with a whole host of other messages, it is more likely to achieve recognition and understanding if it keeps saying the same things in the same sort of tone than if it keeps saying different things. The benefit of consistency therefore is economy of communication – your message costs less to communicate. Although there is little direct statistical evidence to support this assertion, just consider the world's top brands: McDonald's, Coca-Cola, Mercedes Benz and Microsoft, and the degree to which they are consistent in their advertising, identity, product and service.

An inclusive approach to communications is concerned with integration: ensuring that all messages whether they be overt marketing communications, the behaviour of individuals or the quality of services and products, are consistent. The chief barrier to this is the problem of organisational fragmentation. The inclusive approach to communications encompasses a diverse group of people. To overcome fragmentation requires a willingness to work at horizontal communications, so that people have a broad perspective of organisational goals, rather than just a focus on the activities of their business unit, and a willingness to put together cross-functional teams that are concerned with communications in its most catholic interpretation rather than simply advertising or PR. Many organisations are struggling with this problem, but the evidence of the companies that are tackling the issue head on is that there are benefits to be reaped.

The final aspect of the complete corporate brand is interaction. To ensure products and services meet the needs of people and that communications are relevant, organisations need to be good at building relationships with their audiences. They need to listen to the thoughts and suggestions of investors and analysts, the buyer behaviour of consumers, the opinions of local communities and the criticisms of the media. With tightly defined audiences, such as journalists or investors, the relationship should be an open and personal one where information is exchanged to the benefit of all. With larger audiences, such as consumers or individual shareholders, the personal approach has to be substituted for more indirect means, such as advertising, PR and direct marketing. Nonetheless organisations should seek to understand these audiences as best they can through monitoring sales patterns, conducting research and encouraging responses. Organisations may never achieve particularly deep relationships with mass audiences, but they can create an empathy which not only means more appropriate products and messages, but also more informed decision making. Except for the sophisticated few, most organisations simply do not use the information they receive to build relationships sustained by long-term mutual advantage. The secret of building an effective corporate brand isn't complex, it's through doing simple things well: listening to and involving people, informing them, building relationships and integrating internal and external communications. The difficult bit is adapting existing structures and cultures to achieve this simplicity.

Notes

1 The Corporate Brand

1. R. Barthes, *Mythologies* (Paladin, 1989 edn), p. 18.
2. J. Balmer, Corporate Branding and Connoisseurship', *Journal of General Management*, 21(1) (Autumn 1995), p. 24.
3. S. King, *Developing New Brands* (JWT, 1984 edn), p. iii.
4. I. Murdoch, *Metaphysics as a Guide to Morals* (Penguin, 1992). pp. 1, 2.
5. L. Early and G. Mercer, 'The showroom as an assembly line', *EIU International Motor Business* (January 1993).
6. D. Peppers and M. Rogers, *The One to One Future: Building Business Relationships One Customer at a Time* (Piatkus, 1994).
7. W. H. Grant and L. A. Schlesinger, 'Realise Your Customers' Full Potential', *Harvard Business Review* (September/October 1995), p. 60.
8. Interview with author, May 1996.
9. N. Ind, *Terence Conran – The Authorized Biography* (Sidgwick & Jackson, 1995), pp. 160–1.
10. J. Entine, 'Let Them Eat Brazil Nuts', *Dollars and Sense* (March/April 1996), p. 35.
11. RSA, *Tomorrow's Company* (1995), p. 22.
12. D. Usborne, 'Heineken bows out of £20m Burma deal', *The Independent* (11 July 1996).

2 The Corporate Environment

1. P. York, 'Signs of the Times', *Independent on Sunday* (26 November 1995). p. 8.
2. *Financial Times* (4 January 1996), p. 13.
3. *Financial Times* Review of 'The End of the Nation State' (4 January 1996), p. 12.
4. C. Fombrun, *Reputation: Realizing the Value from the Corporate Image* (Harvard Business School Press, 1996), p. 68.
5. M. Suzman, 'Business in the Community A Fine Act to Follow' (*Financial Times*, 1995), p. 4.
6. Fombrun, *Reputation*, p. 131.
7. F. Fukuyama, *Trust: The Social Virtues and the Creation of Prosperity* (Hamish Hamilton, 1995), pp. 335–6.
8. R. Snowdon, 'Mood of the Nation', *Marketing* (4 January 1996), p. 16.
9. Snowdon, 'Mood of the Nation', p. 17.

10. M. Porter, *Competitive Strategy: Techniques for Analyzing Industries and Competitors* (Free Press, 1980), p. 170.
11. *Brands: An International Review by Interbrand* (Mercury Books, 1990), p. 30.
12. A. Mackiewicz, *Guide to Building a Global Image* (EIU/McGraw-Hill, 1993), p. 1.
13. D. Manners, 'Have we had our chips?', *Computer Age* (5 May 1996), p. 24.
14. P. Cochrane, 'The Information Wave', presentation at the first Institute of Direct Marketing Symposium (29 June 1995).
15. Cochrane, 'The Information Wave'.
16. K. Ohmae, *The Borderless World – Power and Strategy in the Interlinked Economy* (Collins, 1990), p. 31.
17. F. Fukuyama, *Trust*, p. 353.
18. Henley Centre for Forecasting (1995).
19. Eurostat (1991).
20. D. Bowen, 'In Japan's UK Outposts, the Natives are Restless', *Independent on Sunday* (19 May 1996), Business, p. 1.
21. M. Jacques, 'Hunting Down the Asian Tigers', *The Independent* (20 May 1996), p. 15.
22. Jacques, 'Hunting Down the Asian Tigers'.
23. S. Huntington, 'The west and the rest', *Prospect* (February 1997), pp. 35, 37.
24. Loyalty is when someone speaks highly of or would recommend a company if asked. Advocacy is when someone speaks highly of or would recommend a company without being asked.

3 Corporate Strategy and the Corporate Brand

1. *Brands: An International Review by Interbrand* (Mercury Business Books, 1990), p. 92.
2. A. Rajan, 'Manufacturing Winners: Becoming World Class in an Anti-Manufacturing Culture', *RSA Journal*, 144(5469) (May 1996), p. 35.
3. E. Schein, *Organizational Culture and Leadership* (Jossey Bass, 1985), p. 273.
4. J. B. Strasser and L. Becklund, *The Story of Nike and the Men Who Played There* (Harcourt Brace Jovanovich, 1991), p. 59.
5. Strasser and Becklund, *The Story of Nike*.
6. David Potter, interview with author (May 1996).
7. Schein, *Organizational Culture*, p. 276.
8. J. Gray, *Managing the Corporate Image* (Quorum Books, 1986), pp. 25–66.
9. S. Greyser, 'Corporate Reputation and the Bottom Line', Speech at the launch of the International Corporate Identity Group, House of Lords (24 January 1996).
10. D. Drennan, 'Down the Organisation', *Management Today* (June 1988).

4 Analysing the Corporate Brand

1. R. Abratt, 'A New Approach to the Corporate Image Management Process', *Journal of Marketing Management*, 5(1) (1989), pp. 63–76.
2. H. J. Stuart, 'Exploring the Corporate Identity/Corporate Image Interface', paper presented at the first Symposium on Corporate Identity Management, University of Strathclyde (16 June 1994).
3. Pastor Wolfgang Helbig, 'The "company" Henriettenstiftung', in K. Schmidt (ed.), *The Quest for Identity* (Cassell, 1995), p. 77.
4. N. Ind, *The Corporate Image* (revised edn) (Kogan Page, 1992), p. 19.
5. Helbig, 'The "company" Henriettenstiftung', p. 75.
6. P. Moss and J. Mills, 'London Transport', in K. Schmidt (ed.), *The Quest for Identity* (Cassell, 1995), p. 143.
7. N. Ind, *The Corporate Image*, p. 21.
8. H. Mintzberg,
9. J. M. T. Balmer, 'The Nature of Corporate Identity: An Explanatory Study', paper presented at the 3rd Corporate Identity Symposium, University of Strathclyde (9 July 1996).
10. A. Rajan, 'Manufacturing Winners: Becoming World Class in an Anti-manufacturing Culture', *RSA Journal*, 144(5469) (May 1996), p. 36.
11. R. Higgins and B. Bannister, 'How Corporate Communication of Strategy Affects Share Price', *Long Range Planning* 25(3) (1992), pp. 27–35.
12. S. Greyser, 'Corporate Reputation and the Bottom Line', speech at the launch of the International Corporate Identity Group, House of Lords (24 January 1996).
13. M. Porter, *Competitive Advantage* (Free Press, 1985), p. 408.
14. J. Burton, 'Composite Strategy: The Combination of Collaboration and Competition', *Journal of General Management*, vol. 21, no. 1 (Autumn 1995), p. 2.
15. F. Fukuyama, 'Trust', op. cit. (1995), p. 163.
16. CBI/Arthur D. Little Survey.
17. CBI/Arthur D. Little, ibid, p. 8.
18. CBI/Arthur D. Little, ibid, p. 13.
19. J. Entine, *Business Ethics* (September 1994).
20. M. Suzman, 'A Fine Act to Follow', *Financial Times Business in the Community*, p. 6.

5 Defining a Corporate Branding and Communications Strategy

1. C. Macrae *et al.*, 'An invitation from MELNET 96 to contribute to the "brand learning organisation"', *The Journal of Brand Management*, 3(4) (February 1996), p. 232.
2. Lippincott & Margulies, *Sense 93, Employees and Image* (1992), p. 18.

3. D.A. Aaker, 'Resisting Temptations to Change a Brand Position/ Execution: The Power of Consistency over Time', *Journal of Brand Management*, 3(4) (February 1996), p. 251.
4. N. Ind, *Great Advertising Campaigns* (Kogan Page, 1993), p. 128.
5. E.F. Schumacher, *Small is Beautiful – A Study of Economics as if People Mattered* (Sphere Books, 1974).
6. D. Peppers and Martha Rogers, *The One-to-One Future – Building Business Relationships One Customer at a Time* (Piatkus, 1994), p. 23.
7. J. Horovitz and N. Kumar, 'Getting Close to the Customer' (*Financial Times, Mastering Management*, Part 13, 1995), p. 2.

6 Employees and Communication

1. R. Trapp, 'We Drill, you do the Rest', *The Independent* (28 Novembe 1996), Tabloid. p. 15.
2. C. Handy, *The Empty Raincoat* (Hutchinson, 1994), p. 160.
3. Lippincott & Margulies, *Sense 93, Employees and Image* (1992), p. 15.
4. C. Handy, *The Empty Raincoat*, p. 74.
5. F. Fukuyama, *Trust: The Social Virtues and the Creation of Prosperity* (Hamish Hamilton, 1995), p. 341.
6. RSA, *Tomorrow's Company* (1995), p. 14.
7. Reed Selection Seminar Series, *Working Towards the Future* (2 March 1995).
8. RSA, *Tomorrow's Company* (1995), p. 16.
9. K. Ohmae, *The Mind of the Strategist* (Penguin, 1983), p. 224.
10. C. Fombrun, *Reputation: Realizing Value from the Corporate Image* (Harvard Business School Press, 1996).
11. Interview with author, February 1997.
12. D. McGregor, 'Theory X and Theory Y', in D.S. Pugh (ed.), *Organization Theory*, 2nd edn (Penguin, 1985), p. 332.
13. M. Peiperi, 'Does Empowerment Deliver the Goods?' (*Financial Times, Mastering Management*, Part 10, 1995), p. 2.
14. M. Peiperi, 'Does Empowerment Deliver the Goods?', p. 4.
15. I. Griffiths, 'The Proud and the Powerful of ICI', *Independent on Sunday* (27 October 1996), Business, p. 4.
16. P. Cappelli and N. Rogovsky,'What Do New Systems Demand of Employees?', (*Financial Times, Mastering Management*, Part 5) (1995).
17. M. Porter, *Competitive Advantage: Creating and Sustaining Superior Performance* (The Free Press, 1985), p. 319.
18. K. Ohmae, *The Mind of the Strategist* (Penguin, 1986), p. 223.
19. C.A. Bartlett and S. Ghoshal, 'Changing the Role of Top Management: Beyond Strategy to Purpose', *Harvard Business Review* (November–December 1994), p. 81.

20. Bartlett and Ghoshal, 'Changing the Role of Top Management', p. 86.
21. F. Mann, 'Studying and Creating Change: A Means to Understanding Social Organisation Research', in C. Arensberg *et al.*, *Industrial Human Relations: A Critical Appraisal* (Harper & Bros, 1957).
22. A. de Geus, 'Companies: What are They?', *RSA Journal*, 143(5460) (June 1995), p. 27.
23. C. Argyris and D. Schon, 'Organizational Learning', in D. Pugh (ed.), *Organizational Theory*, 2nd edn (Pelican, 1985), p. 369.

7 Communicating with Financial Audiences

1. C. Fombrun, *Reputation: Realizing Value from the Corporate Image* (Harvard Business School Press, 1996), p. 193.
2. R. Higgins and J. Diffenbach, 'Communicating Corporate Strategy – The Payoffs and the Risks', *Long Range Planning*, 22(3) (1989), pp. 133–9.
3. RSA, *Tomorrow's Company* (1995), p. 18.
4. R. Trapp, 'The figures must add up, but it's people who count', *Independent on Sunday* (24 November 1996), p. 8.
5. Interview with author, May 1996.
6. RSA, *Tomorrow's Company* (1990), p. 20.
7. F. Fukuyama, *Trust: The Social Virtues and the Creation of Prosperity* (Hamish Hamilton, 1995), pp. 213–14.
8. D. Bence, K. Hapeshi and R. Hussey, 'Examining Investment Information Sources for Sophisticated Investors Using Cluster Analysis', *Accounting and Business Research*, 26(1) (1995), pp. 19–26.
9. E. Vlessing, 'A Rose by any other Corporate Image Might Smell Different', *Financial Weekly* (26 January 1990), p. 20.
10. R. Trapp, 'The Figures must add up, but it's People who Count', *Independent on Sunday* (24 November 1996), p. 8.
11. KPMG, *UK Environmental Reporting Survey* (1994), p. 1.
12. P. Argenti, R. Hansen and S. Neslin, *The Name Game: How Corporate Name Changes Affect Stock Price Tuck Today*.
13. Argenti *et al.*, *The Name Game.*
14. N. Harlan, *McKesson – The Corporate Name: Asset or Liability* (Anspach Grossman, 199).
15. Quoted in Rodgers (n. 17).
16. P. Rodgers, 'Sometimes it's best to let Sleeping Shares Lie', *Independent on Sunday* (1 December 1996), p. 4.

8 Mergers, De-mergers and Strategic Alliances

1. M. Porter, *Competitive Advantage: Creating and Sustaining Superior Performance* (Free Press, 1985), p. 530.

2. A. McDonagh Bengtsson, *Managing Mergers and Acquisitions* (Gower, 1992), p. 9.
3. T. L. Doorley, III, *Making International Strategic Alliances Work* (The Conference Board, 1994), pp. 21–2.
4. Doorley, *Making International Strategic Alliances Work*, p. 20.
5. Doorley, *Making International Strategic Alliances Work*, p. 21.
6. Jones R. Houghton, *Corning's Alliances: 70 Years of Joint Ventures* (The Conference Board, 1994), pp. 20 and 31.
7. J. Bleeke and D. Ernst, *Collaborating to Compete – Using Strategic Alliance and Acquisitions in the Global Marketplace* (Wiley, 1993), pp. 15–16.
8. E. Schein, *Organizational Culture and Leadership* (Jossey-Bass, 1985), p. 35.
9. J. R. Houghton, *Corning's Alliances: 70 Years of Joint Ventures* (The Conference Board, 1994), p. 31.
10. R. Schoenberg, N. Denuelle and D. Norburn, 'National Conflict within European Alliances', *European Business Journal* (1985), p. 8.
11. R. Moss Kanter, 'Collaborative Advantage', *Harvard Business Review* (July–August 1994), p. 101.
12. M. Marks and P. Mirvis, 'The Merger Syndrome', *Psychology Today* (October 1986).
13. McDonagh Bengtsson, *Managing Mergers*, p. 37.
14. Moss Kanter, 'Collaborative Advantage', *Harvard Business Review* (July–August 1994), p. 105.
15. J. Bleeke and D. Ernst, 'The Way to Win in Cross-Border Alliances', *Harvard Business Review* (November–December 1991), p. 135.
16. R. Walker, 'Making an Alliance Work', *Business International* (1990), p. 62.

9 The Global Brand

1. P. Townley, *Making International Strategic Alliances Work* (The Conference Board, 1994), pp. 8–9.
2. P. Kotler and G. Armstron, *Marketing – An Introduction*, 3rd edn (Prentice Hall, 1993), p. 13.
3. S. Huntington, 'The West and the Rest', *Prospect* (February 1997), p. 38.
4. F. Fukuyama, *The End of History and the Last Man* (Penguin, 1992), p. 275.
5. F. Fukuyama, *The End of History*, p. 275.
6. R. Silman and R. Poustie, 'What they Eat, Buy, Read and Watch', *Admap* (July/August 1994), p. 26.
7. Henley Centre/Research International, *Frontiers, 1994/95*.
8. J. Denfield Wood, 'Culture is not Enough', (*Financial Times*, *Mastering Management*, Part 7, 1995), p. 2.
9. G. Hofstede, *Culture's Consequences* (Sage Publications, 1980).

10. F. Fukuyama, *Trust: The Social Virtues and the Creation of Prosperity* (Hamish Hamilton, 1995).
11. J. Denfield Wood, 'Culture is not Enough', (*Financial Times*, *Mastering Management*, Part 7, 1995).
12. Schein, *Organizational Culture and Leadership* (Jossey Bass, 1985), p. 99.
13. A. Mackiewicz, *Guide to Building a Global Image* (EIU/McGraw-Hill, 1994), p. 7.
14. A. Mitchell, 'Brands Play for Global Domination', *Marketing Week* (2 February 1996), p. 2.
15. R. Schoenberg, N. Denuelle and D. Norburn, 'National Conflict within European Alliances', *European Business Journal* (1995), p. 15.
16. Chiat/Day, *The First Twenty Years* (Rizzoli, 1990).
17. P. Kotler and G. Armstrong, *Marketing – An Introduction*, 3rd edn (Prentice-Hall, 1993).
18. Mackiewicz, *Guide to Building a Global Image*, p. 4.

10 Managing the Corporate Brand

1. C. Fombrun, *Reputation: Realizing Value from the Corporate Image*, quoting Alan Towers (Harvard Business School Press, 1996), p. 197.
2. Simon Ingman, interview with author (February 1997).
3. Ind Associates, *Design Management Benchmarking Study*, 1996.
4. C. Macrae, *The Brand Chartering Handbook* (EIU/Addison-Wesley, 1996), p. 322.
5. J. Flint, 'Chrysler', *Forbes Magazine* (January 13 1997), p. 84.
6. C. Argyris, *Intervention Theory and Method* (Addison-Wesley, 1970).
7. R. Moss Kanter, 'Collaborative Advantage', *Harvard Business Review* (July–August 1994), p. 107.
8. E. Schein, *Organizational Culture and Leadership* (Jossey Bass, 1985), p. 243.

11 Conclusion

1. J. Plender, 'A Stake of One's Own', *Prospect* (February 1997), p. 2.

Bibliography

Barthes, R., *Mythologies* (Paladin, 1973).

Fombrun, C., *Reputation: Realizing Value from the Corporate Image* (Harvard Business School Press, 1996).

Fukuyama, F., *The End of History and the Last Man* (Penguin, 1992).

Fukuyama, F., *Trust: The Social Virtues and the Creation of Prosperity* (Hamish Hamilton, 1995).

Ind, N., *The Corporate Image* (revised edn) (Kogan Page, 1992).

Kay, J., *Foundations of Corporate Success* (Oxford University Press, 1995).

Kennedy, P., *Preparing for the Twenty First Century* (Fontana Press, 1994).

Mackiewicz, A., *Guide to Building a Global Image* (EIU/McGraw-Hill, 1993).

Macrae, C., *The Brand Chartering Handbook* (EIU/Addison-Wesley, 1996).

Ohmae, K., *The Borderless World – Power and Strategy in the Interlinked Economy* (Collins, 1990).

Peppers, D. and Rogers, M., *The One-to-One Future – Building Business Relationships One Customer at a Time* (Piatkus, 1994).

Porter, M., *Competitive Strategy: Techniques for Analyzing Industries and Competitors* (The Free Press, 1980).

Porter, M., *Competitive Advantage: Creating and Sustaining Superior Performance* (The Free Press, 1985).

Schein, E., *Organizational Culture and Leadership* (Jossey Bass, 1985).

Schmidt, K. (ed.), *The Quest for Identity* (Cassell, 1995).

Schumacher, E. F., *Small is Beautiful – A Study of Economics as if People Mattered* (Sphere Books, 1974).

Van Riel, C., *Principles of Corporate Communication* (Prentice-Hall, 1995).

Index